BIOGRAPHY OF A FRONTIERSMAN

Simon Kenton
Unlikely Hero

Karen Meyer

Sable CREEK PRESS

Other novels authored by Karen Meyer

  Conflict at Chillicothe   Whispers at Marietta

  Battle at Blue Licks   North to Freedom

  Missing at Marietta   The Tiara Mystery

Visit the author's website ohiofrontierhistorylady.com

Copyright © 2018 by Karen Meyer

All rights reserved. No part of this publication may be reproduced or transmitted in any form or by any means, electronic or mechanical, including recording, photocopying, or by any retrieval system or information storage except for brief quotations in printed reviews, without written permission of the publisher.

Cover art: *Simon Kenton Runs the Gauntlet* and *Simon Kenton, Shawnee Prisoner* courtesy Steve White Art. Copyright Steve White. Used by permission.

Cover and text design by Diane King, dkingdesigner.com

Scripture taken from the King James Version. Public domain.

Published by Sable Creek Press
sablecreekpress.com

ISBN 9780999115763

Names: Meyer, Karen, 1943-
Title: Simon Kenton, unlikely hero : biography of a frontiersman / Karen Meyer.
Description: [Glendale, Arizona] : Sable Creek Press, [2018] | Interest age level: 008-012. | Includes bibliographical references. | Summary: "Simon Kenton first came to Kentucky in 1772 as a teen fleeing justice. The land captivated his heart and he dedicated the next 28 years to helping settlers, fighting Indians, and scouting for famous military leaders."--Provided by publisher.
Identifiers: ISBN 9780999115749 (paperback) | 9780999115763 (hardcover) | ISBN 9780999115756 (ebook)
Subjects: LCSH: Kenton, Simon, 1755-1836--Juvenile literature. | Scouts (Reconnaissance)--Ohio River Valley--Biography--Juvenile literature. | Pioneers--Ohio River Valley--Biography--Juvenile literature. | Ohio River Valley--History--To 1795--Juvenile literature. | Northwest, Old--History--1775-1865--Juvenile literature. | CYAC: Kenton, Simon, 1755-1836. | Scouts (Reconnaissance)--Ohio River Valley--Biography. | Pioneers--Ohio River Valley--Biography. | Ohio River Valley--History--To 1795. | Northwest, Old--History--1775-1865. | LCGFT: Biographies.
Classification: LCC F517.K383 M49 2018 (print) | LCC F517.K383 (ebook) | DDC 976.902092--dc23

Printed in the United States of America.

To Simon Kenton
"...kept by the power of God..."
1 Peter 1:5.

Contents

Introduction 9
1 Fight and Flight 10
2 Simon Butler, Scout 16
3 Simon Butler Begins to Claim Land 20
4 Indian Trouble 25
5 A Bold Plan 30
6 A Momentous Year 35
7 A Trip to Detroit 45
8 Home to Kentucky 49
9 Clark to the Rescue 54
10 Revolutionary War Battles 57
11 Simon's Homecoming 61
12 Building Kenton's Station 65
13 From Wilderness to Settled Land 70
14 The Greenville Treaty 74
15 Simon, Landowner in Two States 77
16 Tecumseh 80
17 Simon on the Move 83
18 Simon at Camp Meeting 87
19 War Declared 89
20 The Fifty-Year Reunion 96
Glossary of Unfamiliar Terms 101
Time Line 104
Bibliography for Simon Kenton, Unlikely Hero 107
Endnotes 109
Image Credits 112

Karen Meyer

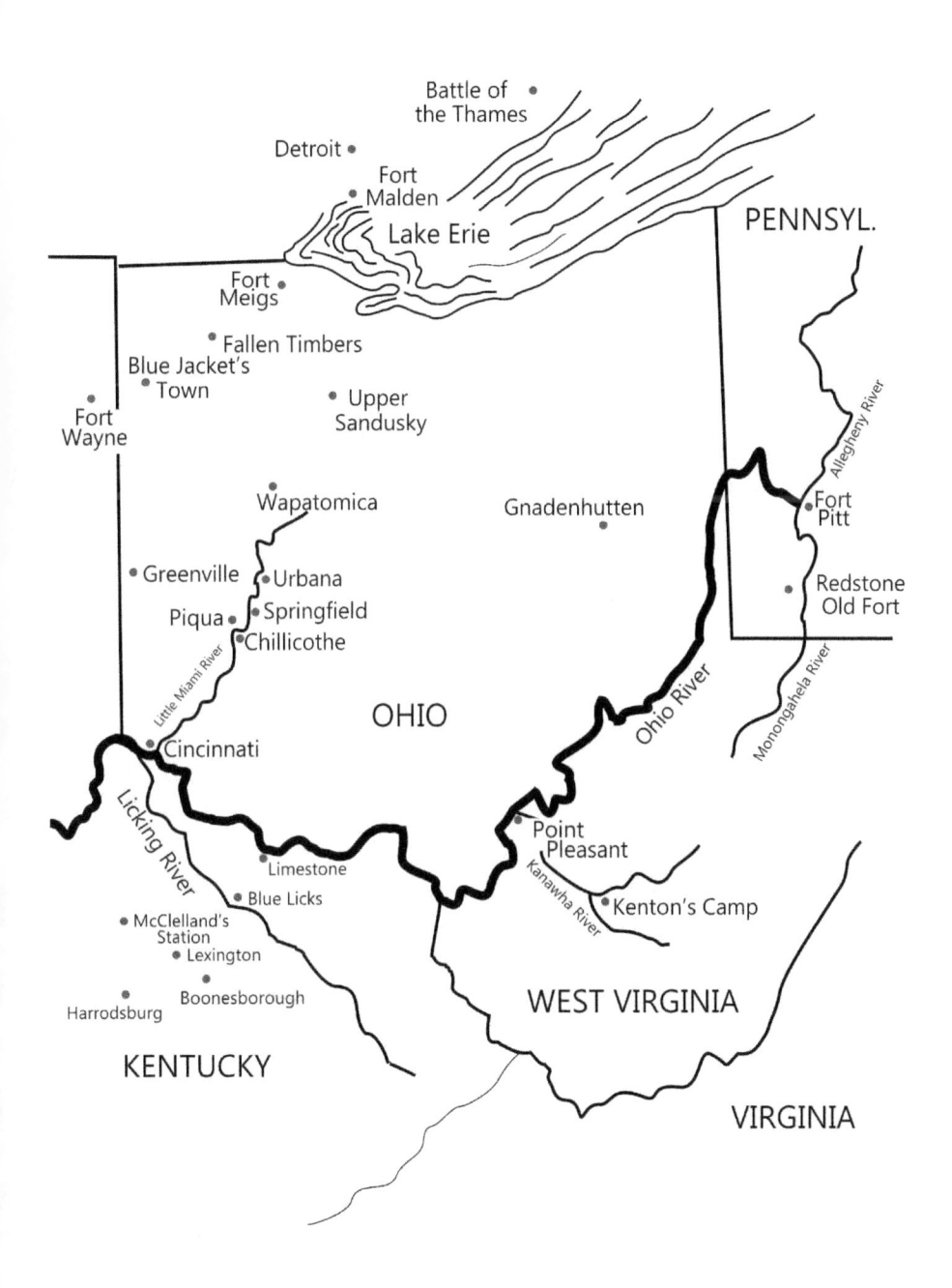

Simon Kenton Unlikely Hero

Introduction

Some men leave a trail of letters and documents for researchers and biographers to mine for details and quotations. Simon Kenton did not. He never learned to read or write, even though he eventually could shape the loops and curves of his own name to sign a document.

Simon knew the great men and influenced many major events of his time. Thus he left a trail of sorts, like that of the wild animals or the Indians he could track so well. He left his mark on the people he met. We will follow this trail and meet some of the men and women who knew him. Through them we will get to know this man who had such an unlikely start toward the life of fame and service he lived.

1
Fight and Flight

Virginia, 1771

The two young men struggled with each other in the woods, grunting as they traded blows. Only forest creatures watched this bare-knuckle fight. William Leachman, about twenty years of age, gained the upper hand early, and anyone watching would have bet his money on him. But the fire of first love fueled Simon Kenton's fists. Leachman had married the girl Simon had chosen. Simon burned for revenge and vowed he would thrash the older and taller man. Now he gritted his teeth, remembering the humiliating loss when he fought Leachman a year ago.

Simon, ducking punches and rolling, angled his opponent toward a small bush. With a shout, he grabbed William by his hair and wrapped his long ponytail around the branches. Now Simon gave free rein to his temper and punched the man in the face again and again, until his opponent lay still.

Simon stared at the man sprawled on the ground before him. He tried to revive him with water from a nearby stream, but his rival did not move. Simon's anger turned to horror. Was Leachman dead?

Simon raced away from the awful scene and hid until dark. He fingered the moles on his neck—was it just superstition or did they prove he would hang someday? He gulped as he felt the noose tightening. A vivid picture of a hanging he had witnessed flashed through his mind.

Murderers in Virginia always met speedy justice. He could never return home. His parents were God-fearing people and would never shelter a killer.

Simon Kenton Unlikely Hero

So Simon, the seventh child of Mark and Mary Kenton, turned his back on the **tenant farm** in Virginia where he'd been born sixteen years before. Hatless and shoeless, he fled for his life.

After Simon crossed the boundary of his own Fauquier County, hunger drove him to stop at outlying farms. He hated farm work and had vowed never to spend his life with a hoe in his hand. Now he worked for a meal and a spot to sleep. Simon faced a turning point. To stay alive, he was forced to change from the lazy boy who would rather wander in the woods than work. No more picking fights or playing practical jokes. He would start a new life by disappearing into the wilderness.

Simon already had a destination in mind. He had thrilled at his Uncle Thomas's stories about a wondrous land called the **Middle Ground**. The uncle, an Indian fur trader, had ventured down the Ohio River and lived to tell about it. Many Indian tribes shared that fertile land for a hunting ground. Tales of woods full of game and streams full of fish aroused Simon's imagination. But Uncle Thomas added a warning. "A man can lose his life there, and many have already."

Simon yearned to see the Middle Ground with his own eyes. There he could stop looking over his shoulder for the sheriff, since no one enforced the law.

By the time he had tramped the one hundred sixty weary miles to Warm Springs, Virginia, Simon had a plan. He knocked on the door of the town miller, Jacob Butler. Simon had learned about this prosperous widower from his previous stop.

He introduced himself as Simon *Butler*, hoping he might be taken for a distant relative. If Mr. Butler hired him, he could earn enough to buy the gun, powder, and provisions he would need for the wilderness.

Jacob welcomed the young stranger. He not only hired Simon, he treated him almost like a son. Simon worked hard at Butler's mill for nearly two months. He saved his wages and bought much of what he needed for the Middle Ground. Jacob presented Simon with a fine flintlock longrifle, essential to survival on the frontier. Simon swallowed a lump in his throat as he said goodbye to this kind man. The wilderness lands called his name. They beckoned Simon *Butler*.

How Longrifles Settled the Frontier

Without the longrifle, settlers would have starved and been driven out of Indian lands. These guns, about five feet long, shot a single lead ball, very accurate to 100 yards or more. (In contrast, a musket, which had no grooves inside the barrel, was accurate to 50 yards.) The rifle-shooter first poured a charge of black powder inside the long barrel. He (or she) then used a hickory rod to ram down a lead ball wrapped in a greased patch. A small amount of black powder went into a tiny pan at the base of the outside of the barrel. This powder was ignited by a flint striking the steel plate next to the pan. The fire exploded the charge of powder through a small hole at the base of the barrel. Does this sound complicated? It was! The powder wouldn't work if it were damp, so frontiersmen were warned, "keep your powder dry".

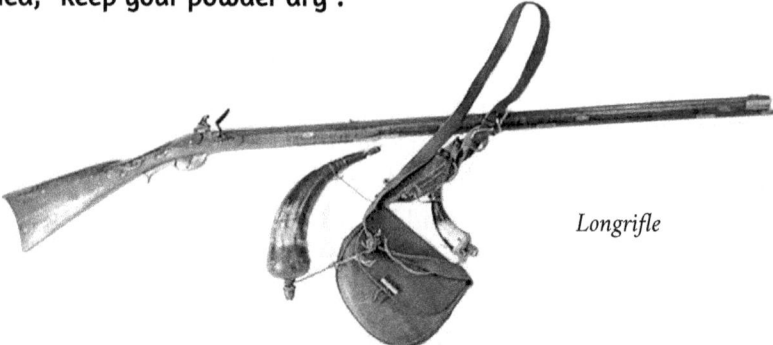

Longrifle

With rising excitement, Simon headed north to Fort Pitt in western Pennsylvania, more than five hundred miles away. Fort Pitt, where the Ohio River began, drew Simon like a magnet. In this frontier town he could find other men heading to the wild country along the river.

Simon linked his fortunes with two other adventurers crazy enough to explore the Middle Ground. John Yeager, an older man and experienced woodsman, spun tales like Uncle

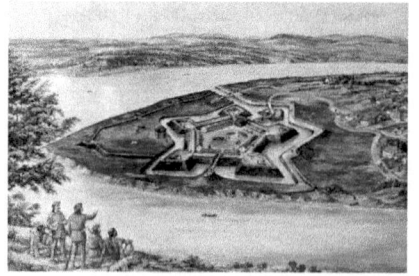

Fort Pitt at Junction of Monongahela and Allegheny Rivers

Simon Kenton Unlikely Hero

Thomas's stories, whetting Simon's appetite for a **long hunt**. Yeager also mentioned seeing stands of cane in the Middle Ground. This bamboo-like plant indicated rich ground. Yeager had lived with Indians from an early age, knew their languages, and excelled in tracking game. George Strader, a greenhorn close to Simon's age, was as eager as Simon to explore the Kentucky[1] hunting grounds.

As John Yeager mapped a plan for a year-long hunt in the wilderness, Simon's eyes sparkled. He'd been dreaming of the Middle Ground for months. The three men loaded their supplies—blankets, extra shirts, parched corn, jerky, traps, rifles and ammunition—into their dugout canoe. Just as the leaves began to show fall colors, they set off down the Ohio River.

At a Mingo village, they "frolicked and danced with the young Indians". Simon and George soaked up everything they could about Indian culture, learning to read a trail, and staying alert for dangers. Their lives would depend on these skills.

They paddled down the Ohio River, past the mouth of the Big Sandy River, finally into the Middle Ground! Exploring all along Kentucky's northern border, they searched for fields of cane, but found none. They paddled three hundred miles back upriver and followed a tributary river, the Great Kanawha, inland to make camp. Winter would come soon, so they hurried to set up their three-sided shelter. The three hunters bravely established their camp on the edge of the Middle Ground, the hunting grounds for at least seven tribes of Indians.

Yeager selected a huge fallen tree for their back wall. Simon dragged and lifted fallen logs into place for the two side walls. George filled the gaps with leaves, brush, and dirt. Saplings held up a roof of sod and leaves.

Each evening the men built a cooking fire on the open side of their shelter and roasted their game. Long before the moon rose, they rolled in their blankets and aimed their feet toward the fire. As the night sounds lulled them to sleep, they felt safe and warm.

All winter the two younger men enjoyed hunting and trapping for furs—otter, deer, elk, bear, beaver, and buffalo—while Yeager dressed the pelts at camp. In spring, they piled the furs in the canoe and paddled

13

toward the Ohio. Simon remembered all the landmarks on the way back to the river—the wilderness felt like home. He wanted to stay for another year instead of paddling upstream to sell their furs. Simon grinned when a trader's canoe floated into view. They flagged it down and bartered for clothes, ammunition, and corn, enough for another year of hunting.

They had been safe from Indians for more than a year in their camp. One rainy, cold March evening as a turkey roasted for dinner, they removed their **leggins** and moccasins to dry in front of the fire. A tiny noise made all three men glance up. Simon's heart nearly stopped beating when he saw three Indians with guns aimed at them. The hunters sprang up and ran in three directions.

They heard a shot. Simon shouted at George to meet him at the bear trap. They last glimpsed Yeager facing the Indians, their tomahawks raised.

Hours later, Simon and George met and took stock. They had the shirts on their backs, but no leggins, no moccasins, no guns, and no food.

George shivered, wondering what they could do in this hopeless situation.

Simon warned they could not return to camp. The Indians would be ransacking their supplies and enjoying their turkey dinner.

The two men crawled into a cave and huddled there all night. Before dawn, Simon and George headed toward the Ohio River. They tramped miles through an unfriendly wilderness, always alert for Indians.

After three days without food, the men had spent nearly all their strength. For two more days they crawled, to ease their cut and swollen feet. More than once they wanted to give up. Simon rejoiced when they spotted a man and his wife collecting sap for maple sugar. This couple took care of them for days until they could travel.

George bid Simon goodbye before heading back east. He had lost his taste for exploring. Simon knew he could not stay away from the wilderness, even after their narrow escape. He thrilled at the bounty of deer, elk, buffalo, and bear. He admired the unspoiled beauty of the Middle Ground. Danger made things more exciting.

In the wilderness, a man's reputation spread by word of mouth. Men sat around campfires recounting tales of bravery. As they retold the story

Simon Kenton Unlikely Hero

of the two woodsmen escaping from the Indians, Simon's fame spread. Every time Simon met someone from his home state, he shuddered. They might recognize him. He could not camouflage his red hair, broad shoulders, and six-foot-plus height. Would he face a trial for murder?

Simon soon added another feat of daring and skill to his growing fame. He led an exploring party of fourteen Virginians planning to survey land and build cabins in the Kentucky wilderness. They begged the eighteen-year-old woodsman to guide them through the area, the very place he had already explored.

Simon listened with interest as the surveyors described making "tomahawk improvements". This meant slashing corner trees with your own mark and pounding stakes to claim thousand-acre plots in the wilderness of Virginia. Simon learned to survey so he could claim some of this land for himself.

Simon guided the surveyors on their way back home by canoe up the Ohio River. As they approached the Three Islands, Simon sensed danger, a Shawnee ambush ahead. He insisted they should travel overland back to Virginia instead of on the river. The surveyors argued against the risk of wandering through unmarked wilderness. But Simon showed them, from a safe vantage point, the large party of Indians preparing their attack. With no further grumbling, the men abandoned their canoes and shouldered their packs. Simon led them all safely back to civilization.

The surveyors told stories of this feat as they traveled to Williamsburg, Virginia. They recited tales of young Simon Butler, each time with more Indians, extra dangers, and fiercer wild animals. This fame made Simon even more fearful he would be recognized as Leachman's murderer.

If you had committed a crime, would you run away, or face the consequences?

2
Simon Butler, Scout

1774

Explorers

The great continent of North America has attracted explorers from many nations, including Spanish, French, Dutch, and British. They claimed land and fought each other over the fur trade with the natives. Christopher Columbus called the people Indians, since he thought he had found the sea route to India. The pioneers also called them Indians or used the name of their individual tribe. The term Native American came into use in the 1960s. This term reflects the fact that the various tribes were the natives of this continent and that Europeans were the latecomers.

Simon's scouting skill would soon be in great demand. Indians raided border settlements of Virginia, trying to force the settlers to go back home. Some did, but most built forts for protection, fearing for their lives. Lord Dunmore, Virginia's British governor, declared war on the Shawnee. He called for both regular army and **militia** to muster at Fort Pitt. Simon, always eager for more excitement, reckoned the militia could use his exploring skills.

When nineteen-year-old Simon strode through the fort's gate, his reputation had arrived ahead of him. He signed up with the militia as a scout and messenger. Simon admired his tall commanding officer—another red-haired Virginian, George Rogers Clark.

Simon Kenton Unlikely Hero

British army officers looked down their noses at the militia, a mostly untrained people's army. But Simon and the other buckskin-clad scouts deserved respect, since they acted as eyes and ears for the army as it moved into enemy territory. Some scouts also translated messages to and from the tribal chiefs as needed.

Simon Butler met another Simon who would become a lifelong friend. Simon Girty had spent eight years as an adopted Indian. He knew Indian languages and respected Indian ways. Girty, slightly built and dark-haired, suggested a way to confirm their friendship. The two Simons used a Seneca Indian ceremony to become blood brothers. They nicked their wrists and let their blood mingle. They swore to protect each other, even at the risk of their lives. Neither imagined the future danger looming to test this pledge.

In the spring the troops headed into Indian country on the first skirmish of Lord Dunmore's War against the hostile Shawnee and Mingo tribes. British Colonel Angus McDonald fought well if the enemy stood in a row, but Indians hid behind trees. At the sound of gunfire the Colonel dove under a log! Simon and the militiamen decided McDonald was a coward who feared leading his men into a real battle. They were right. The soldiers rarely shot their muskets; instead they burned Indian villages, destroyed crops, and marched back home. Attacks on the settlers did decrease, for a while.

For the fall campaign Simon reported to a new leader, a militiaman named Colonel Andrew Lewis. Lewis engaged the Indians in a major battle lasting for five agonizing hours. The Battle of Point Pleasant pitted Lewis' army against a thousand Indians under Chief Cornstalk. The Indians crept through the woods to attack the smaller force of militia. Butler and Girty had the dangerous mission of carrying messages before and during the battle. Fierce fighting filled the woods with smoke while death-dealing bullets whizzed back and forth. Neither side would give way. Late in the day, the Indians disappeared. Their scouts had reported British reinforcements marching to the battle.

The British claimed victory, but with seventy-five killed and twice that many injured, they could not afford many such damaging triumphs.

The Shawnee and Mingo called for peace. Everyone met to discuss treaty terms at Camp Charlotte in Ohio country.

Chief Logan of the Mingo refused to attend the peace conference. He had once

Battle of Point Pleasant

been a good friend of the settlers until his whole family was cruelly massacred. Logan had picked up his war tomahawk and led his men in battle. Simon Butler and Simon Girty went to Logan's camp to write down and carry the chief's message to the peace conference.

Logan's Speech

"I appeal to any white man to say if ever he entered Logan's cabin hungry and I gave him not meat; if ever he came cold or naked and I gave him not clothing. Such was my love for the whites that those of my own country pointed at me as I passed and said, 'Logan is the friend of the white man'; I had even thought to have lived with you but for the injuries of one man. [He] . . . murdered all the relatives of Logan, not sparing even my women and children. There runs not a drop of my blood in the veins of any living creature. This called on me for revenge. I have sought it. I have killed many. I have fully glutted my vengeance.

For my country, I rejoice at the beams of peace; but do not harbor the thought that mine is the joy of fear. Logan never felt fear. He will not turn on his heel to save his life.

Who is there to mourn for Logan? Not one."

This eloquent speech moved those who heard it at Camp Charlotte. It became known as Logan's Lament. President Thomas Jefferson included it word for word in his book, *Notes on the State of Virginia*. For one hundred years, youngsters would memorize it from their *McGuffey Readers*.

Scholars praise it as one of the finest examples of Native American oratory.

The Camp Charlotte peace treaty gave Virginia all the land south of the Ohio River, today's states of Kentucky and West Virginia. Now the Middle Ground opened to settlers.

The militia disbanded and the two Simons gladly said goodbye to military life. They parted ways, but knew someday their paths would cross again. Little did they guess what dreadful events would threaten their reunion.

Chief Logan

> **Have you ever met someone who might become a lifelong friend?**

3
Simon Butler Begins to Claim Land

1774-1775

Simon longed to find the cane lands he'd heard about from his Uncle Thomas. He resolved to search again for them. He partnered with someone as eager as he to explore—Thomas Williams, a good hunter and woodsman. In November they set off in high spirits down the Ohio by canoe for a long hunt. A French trader gave them the key to finding their goal. They'd find the cane lands inland from a creek emptying into the Ohio between limestone bluffs.

Indian Buffalo Hunt

Simon Kenton Unlikely Hero

They finally found these vast fields of cane the following spring. The cane stalks, some of them four times as high as a man, waved in a gentle breeze. Simon had never seen anything so delightful. He chose an ideal spot for their camp, on a hill with a clear spring flowing from the side. They cleared an acre in the center of the cane and planted corn. Both men claimed land in the area by slashing their marks in trees.

Simon itched to explore the wilderness, so Williams did most of the farming. Both kept their guns loaded in spite of the Camp Charlotte peace treaty. Simon hiked the Indian war trails, trying to decipher the

sun	day	morning / noon / evening	mountain	river
three nights	three days and three nights	lake	clouds, rain	snake
geese	turtle	buffalo tracks	eagle	many fish
camp	horse	bear alive	bear dead	canoe
dead person	campfire	deer tracks	war	friendship
prayer	man	woman	we	plenty corn
life	death	new moon	half moon	full moon

Indian Pictograms

21

messages painted on trees by the Indians. The mysterious symbols of men, animals, sun, and moon intrigued him. Someday he would find out what they meant.

Simon also tramped the buffalo trace, a hard-packed road wide enough for two horses to ride side by side. (Neither Simon nor Williams owned a horse.) This broad path formed when vast herds of buffalo crossed the Ohio River and headed straight for the salt spring, Blue Licks, about twenty-five miles inland.

One day Simon heard a distant rumble and felt the ground shake. He sprinted to climb a tree before thousands of buffalo thundered past. Across the stream of charging beasts Simon spotted another man up a tree. Was the man friend or foe? When the herd finally disappeared Simon called, "Show yourself!" The man demanded the same of Simon, but it was now clear they were friends, since they spoke the same language.

The man, John Hinkston, told Simon that he and fifteen fellow settlers had each built a cabin not forty miles away. Simon went for a visit and met them all.

Pioneer Cabins

Pioneer cabins measured about twenty by twenty feet square, with a hard-packed dirt floor. Heavy plank doors, barred each night, kept the residents safe. During an Indian attack, defenders stood on benches to reach slots high in the walls for firing rifles. One tiny window used oiled paper instead of glass. The stone fireplace provided heat and light, and often held a kettle of bubbling stew.

Simon Kenton Unlikely Hero

Hundreds of would-be settlers floated down the Ohio River and many of them landed at Limestone Creek. Simon met them, helped them find good land and taught them how to live safely in the wilderness. Now Simon had a purpose in exploring. Guiding newcomers suited him much better than farming.

The settlers flooding into northern Kentucky clashed with Indians again and again. Simon searched for signs of Indian war parties so he could warn the **stations** before a Shawnee attack. His help sometimes made the difference between life and death. Settlers retold stories of how Simon shot the Indian whose tomahawk was poised over someone's head or how he rescued those who had been kidnapped. They appreciated his help as meat-provider, too. This job had benefits for the young hunter; he got good cooking, enjoyed companionship, and had a realistic reason to disappear when strangers arrived. He still felt uneasy about a possible manslaughter charge.

In the spring of 1775 Simon and the settlers received alarming news of big problems brewing. Newcomers alerted the frontier of the British Redcoat attack on the Colonial Militia in Lexington, Massachusetts in April. The thirteen colonies faced a war with Great Britain.

Would You Have Been a Tory or a Patriot?

Not everyone thought the thirteen American colonies should separate from the Mother country, Great Britain. Those who were loyal to King George III were known as Loyalists or Tories. Patriots on the other hand cried, "No taxation without representation." When Boston Patriots threw British tea into the harbor rather than pay tax on it, Britain closed the harbor. This caused great hardship to most of the colonies and hardened opinions against King George. Two and a half years later, on July 4, 1776, the colonies declared their independence.

In the fall of 1775, Simon had the chance to help two men whose canoe had upset in a storm, dumping their gear and nearly drowning them. One man, Hendricks, had determined to stay on the frontier. The other, Fitzpatrick, wanted to go back to Pennsylvania, even if it meant going alone. So Simon and his partner left Hendricks at their Blue Licks salt-making camp and took the other man to their Limestone camp. They helped him build a canoe and gave him a few supplies, and sent him on his way.

When they got back to the Blue Licks camp they found gruesome remains. The camp had been raided and it was clear that Hendricks had met his Maker by way of an Indian tomahawk.

Alarmed, Simon and Williams broke camp and made the rounds of the new settlements—Hinkston's Station, McClelland's Station, Harrodsburg, and Boonesborough. Their warnings of possible Indian attack came as old news to the settlements. These settlements had endured Indians stealing horses, shooting cattle, burning cabins, and worse, killing whole families. Simon and Williams lodged at Hinkston's Station for the winter. This newest and weakest settlement needed their help, both to hunt and to defend against possible attack.

Simon ventured out alone for the dangerous job of winter hunting. He hiked to a site at night and built a tiny fire in a pit, and huddled over it till daylight with his gun at the ready. He carried the fresh-killed deer, sometimes two of them, back to the fort on his shoulders. By late winter, most stations had nothing else to eat except what he provided.

When two sides are at war and you have ties to both, how would you decide which side to join?

4
Indian Trouble

1776-1777

*S*imon and the other settlers knew something had to be done. So many Indian war parties were attacking the tiny settlements they would soon be wiped out. The settlers met and chose George Rogers Clark and John Gabriel Jones to beg help from the Virginia Assembly. (Kentucky County made up a huge chunk of the state of Virginia.) The Assembly refused at first—with war looming with Great Britain, they had bigger worries. Clark convinced the Assembly by reminding them, "If a country were not worth protecting, it was not worth claiming." They finally authorized five hundred pounds of gunpowder and lead for bullets.

At Fort Pitt, eight men loaded the precious military supplies in three canoes, as Indian spies watched. They glided down the Ohio River.

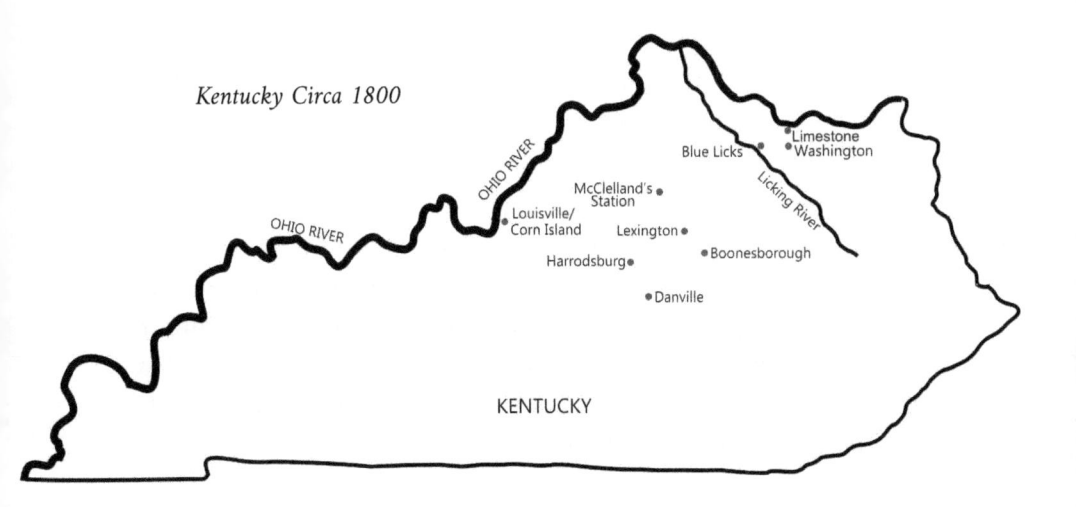

Kentucky Circa 1800

Karen Meyer

Near the Scioto River, five war canoes full of Indians sped out to chase them. The eight men escaped and under cover of night stopped at Three Islands to hide the ammunition in five different places. They proceeded to Limestone Creek, set the canoes adrift, and hiked to find help to bring back the hidden supplies. Simon Butler recruited a group of thirty men for the dangerous task.

But first, tiny McClelland's Station needed their help. The desperate settlers there braced for an expected Shawnee attack. It began at dawn, with fierce fighting on both sides. Before the sun was high, the leaders of both sides had been killed. John McClelland had been felled by a bullet to his head, and Mohawk Chief Pluggy lay dead with two bullets in his chest.

The Indians rode off carrying their dead chief. Was the retreat a trick to draw them out of the fort? Simon and another man trailed the attackers to the Ohio. They hid in thick underbrush to make sure the painted warriors did cross the river. When the coast was clear, Simon and his partner paddled downstream to make sure the hidden powder and lead were still safe.

Simon and his men collected and delivered the powder and lead, but the situation in the frontier settlements still got worse. Fear drove the families away from the land they'd cleared and the cabins they'd built. Forts were safer, but sometimes too many people crowded in and food supplies ran low. Many families headed back east so the smallest settlements had to be abandoned. Together the two largest ones, Harrodsburg and Boonesborough, had only one hundred and three men able to fight.

Governor Patrick Henry promoted George Rogers Clark to the rank of major and gave him command of the militia of the newly-formed Kentucky County, (still part of Virginia.) Clark had the difficult task of defending the frontier settlements. He selected Simon Butler as one of five men to spy on the Indians, knowing his skill would help the settlers prepare for an attack. Now Simon received pay for something he did anyway.

For Simon and the others on the frontier, the distant Revolutionary War battles sparked no fear. But soon enough the battles spread from the eastern states. The British recruited Indians as allies, supplying them guns and powder to use against the settlers.

Simon Kenton Unlikely Hero

Daniel Boone Led Settlers Overland to Kentucky

Daniel Boone came to the frontier with his family across the mountains in 1775 and founded one of the earliest settlements. Boonesborough's double row of cabins with picketing formed a rectangle, with blockhouses at each corner. Three Shawnee sieges of the fort lasted many days.

The Kentucky frontier drew trouble like a magnet. Simon had the talent of being in the right place to help when trouble arose. In early spring of 1777 Chief Black Fish and two hundred Shawnee warriors attacked the Harrodsburg settlement. Due to nasty March weather, they abandoned the siege after three days. Simon guessed Boonesborough would be attacked next. This weaker settlement had just twenty-one men to defend it. Simon made sure he was there to help.

The attack on Boone's settlement came in late April. It began with a few Shawnee warriors attacking two men gathering firewood. Daniel Boone and ten other men raced out to rescue the firewood gatherers from what they thought was a small raiding party. When the rescuers ventured far from the gates of the fort, a hundred Indians poured out of

Fort Boonesborough

27

the woods, cutting off the route to safety. The men feared they would never get back to the fort.

Boone ordered them to fire their rifles, then charge. Battling every inch toward the gate, the men swung empty rifles as clubs or used their tomahawks. Simon led a group from the fort to provide cover for them, using his skill at shooting and reloading on the run. Halfway to the gate, Boone took a rifle ball to his ankle and tumbled down. A Shawnee raised his tomahawk to finish him off. Simon shot the Indian and raced forward, hefting Boone over his shoulder like a sack of grain. Indians still blocked the way to the gate, so Simon knocked them aside using Boone's body. The gate swung open wide enough for them all to rush inside before the defenders slammed it closed and slid the heavy bar in place.

Simon Kenton saving Daniel Boone

Daniel told his young friend, "Well, Simon, you have behaved like a man today. Indeed you are a fine fellow." The feat of saving Daniel Boone's life added one more tale to the Simon Butler legend.

The siege of Boonesborough lasted for three long days. When Black Fish's main force finally disappeared, the settlers cautiously stepped outside their stronghold. Indians still lurked in the forests, stealing horses and killing the cattle. They planned to starve the settlers shut up in the fort.

The settlers had springtime work to do, so some guarded while men and women planted, boiled sugar sap, and built corrals for livestock. Simon helped in the dangerous job of hunting. Any shot to kill a deer might also bring Shawnee warriors to slay the hunter.

Simon warned everyone to expect another siege, so the defenders prepared for it. Men strengthened the stockade and drove the horses and cattle inside the fort walls each night. They feared to plant their gardens without a guard.

Simon Kenton Unlikely Hero

A month later the Shawnee returned for another attack. The fort's men and boys shot from the portholes as women molded bullets and reloaded guns. Under cover of the thick smoke from the black powder, Indians struggled to set fire to the log **palisade.** This failed, to the great relief of the settlers.

Simon crept out at dawn of the third day to see whether the attackers had disappeared. Whoops of joy greeted his shout that they were gone. Besides danger, sieges meant filthy conditions and short rations inside the fort.

Do you think you would enjoy living in a fort in the wilderness?

5
A Bold Plan

May 1778

George Rogers Clark's idea fired Simon's imagination. Clark, leader of the Kentucky militia, guessed the British forts in the west were weak and undermanned. Kaskaskia and Cahokia were French towns seized and fortified by the British government. If Clark could surprise them, they might be captured without a shot. Simon volunteered to scout their defenses, but he drew the short straw and two other men set off to spy.

George Rogers Clark

The spies returned and confirmed the poor defenses of the forts, so Clark presented his bold plan to Governor Patrick Henry for approval. The governor's permission came with a promotion. Clark rose to Colonel of the Kentucky militia.

Now Clark must raise an army, so he asked Simon Butler to help him. Simon couldn't reveal many details, not even their destination, so many militiamen refused to join the mission. Success depended on surprise, so the men would learn the secret after they were underway.

Simon recruited the few men who could be spared from frontier defense and met Clark and his militia at Corn Island in the Ohio River. When Clark finally revealed the plan of attack, fifty militiamen refused to go along. What a crazy idea—crossing a hundred and twenty miles

Clark's Expedition to Kaskaskia

of British-held territory with no supplies! The rest of the militia, 175 seasoned frontiersmen, prepared to follow Clark on this rough and dangerous mission.

Simon would play a key role in this mission. Clark knew he could depend on his friend's uncanny ability to find the way. He often assigned Simon to the most difficult and dangerous tasks.

Besides Simon's help, Clark had another advantage up his sleeve. He had just received word that France had signed an alliance with the colonials and declared war on England. Clark hoped the French townspeople of Kaskaskia and Cahokia would welcome him.

Though Clark set out with half the force he had planned, his confidence didn't waver. He suggested that their small number might be an advantage in surprising Kaskaskia.

The buckskin-clad army floated down the Ohio River as far as they could, three hundred miles. Once on land, they set off across country. Clark forbade any shooting game for food, afraid to attract the attention of the many tribes of Indians in the area. The men found blackberries but little else to add to their rations of parched corn and jerky.

Two English-speaking hunters happened along and were pressed to join the expedition. Clark pumped them for current **intelligence** about Kaskaskia. The British commander there, Philippe Rocheblave, had militia but no regular army. One bit of information helped Clark form a plan. British propaganda described Virginians as savages and barbarians waving long knives. Clark believed he could scare the French townspeople into submission with his fierce little army.

One of the hunters said he knew the way, so the hungry army followed him through swampy wilderness for three days. When they reached the prairie, the guide lost his bearings. A furious Colonel Clark threatened to hang him. Besides being hungry, the men were hot, mosquito-bitten, and tired, and now their mission hung in the balance. The prairie offered no cover in case of Indian attack and perhaps this guide had led them into a trap.

Simon convinced Clark to give the guide a chance instead of killing him on the spot. The frightened man did discover the route and led them to the wide Kaskaskia River where it met the Mississippi. We can imagine how the ragtag army's spirits rose as they saw their goal ahead. Would they be able to surprise the soldiers guarding the fort jutting up in the center of the town? Clark outlined the plan for his captains. Under cover of night they would sneak across the river into the peaceful town of Kaskaskia. He charged them—no looting, no roughness toward men or women, and don't even talk to the townspeople. Keep the army marching around the town, to appear a thousand strong. This fierce show of force might capture the fort without a shot.

They crossed the river by boat and split into three groups. One group surrounded the town and a second group followed Clark to confront the militia.

Simon Butler led a third small group on the toughest assignment. He and a few others charged right into Commander Rocheblave's bedroom. Simon shook him awake and roared that he was now a prisoner of the Americans under Colonel George Rogers Clark. The commandant, nicknamed "Roseblock" by Clark's men, opened his eyes to a huge frontiersman waving a rifle. It must be a nightmare. How could those words be true?

The townspeople were in a tumult, fearing for their lives from these terrifying **long knives** marching through town. But when they understood the situation, they lined up to sign the oath of allegiance to the new nation. The British militia, about a hundred and fifty men, surrendered without a fight. By dawn, all was quiet. Later, nearby Cahokia also fell without a shot fired. Clark and his Kentucky militia had pulled off an amazing feat.

British-held French towns

The French-Canadian towns of Kaskaskia, Cahokia, and Vincennes became British outposts during the Revolutionary War. When George Roger's Clark's small army arrived, the townspeople gladly switched allegiance to the American cause. The British ceded the entire Northwest Territory to the United States in the 1783 Treaty of Paris.

Clark next set his sights on Vincennes, the British fort two hundred miles closer to Kentucky. If they failed to capture it, the Illinois country, as well as Kentucky, could be lost to the British. They must act quickly before the British commander in Detroit, Henry Hamilton, sent reinforcements to this distant outpost. Clark determined to build on this latest victory for the young nation. He sent young Simon Butler and two others to spy the strength of Vincennes.

Would you have signed up for the dangerous expedition with George Rogers Clark or stayed safely at home?

6
A Momentous Year

September 1778

*S*imon excelled at spying and this time was more fun than usual. Vincennes, a small British outpost in Indiana, had no idea they were being spied on. Years later Simon recounted the story this way: "Clark started me, Shadrach Bond and Elisha Batty for the purpose of viewing Fort Vincennes. We came, and hid our hats and guns . . . and then at night came back and walked the streets with the Indians and the French, with our blankets around us and tomahawks concealed . . . for three nights." We can imagine the three men enjoying their masquerade as they blended in with the local townspeople and the Indians trading at the fort. It was a simple task to gather information about Vincennes' strength, or lack of it.

The other two spies returned to Clark, but Simon reported to Colonel Bowman, the regular army officer now leading Kentucky's militia. Bowman was not interested whatsoever in attacking the British outpost. He thought he could gain more glory by attacking Indians, so he sent Simon and two others on the dangerous task of scouting the major Shawnee village of Chillicothe.

The Shawnee Tribe Was Divided into Five Bands

The Shawnee warrior chief must be chosen from the Chillicothe (or Chalagawtha) band, who called his village by the same name. When the chief died, the new chief's village would again be called "Chillicothe". That's why Ohio has many Shawnee Chillicothe villages. After the

35

Early Settlements and Indian Villages

Simon Kenton Unlikely Hero

Greenville Treaty opened Ohio to settlement, a new Chillicothe grew along the Scioto River. It became Ohio's first capital.

Chillicothe's **wegiwas** stretched a quarter mile from the Little Miami River to the council house at the top of the hill. The three spies hid in the woods behind the village, scouting out the number of warriors. Simon spotted many stolen horses in the corral. The night before they headed home, they sneaked into the corral. Using salt to attract the horses, they slipped halters on seven of them—one more than they could handle. Simon and the other two men urged the horses to a gallop and headed toward the Ohio River. Shouts erupted from behind them—they had been discovered.

By riding hard, they left the Indians far behind, but another obstacle loomed ahead. Lightning flashed and thunder rumbled as they reached the river. The horses refused to swim across the dark and turbulent water. Simon had a gut feeling they should abandon the horses and save their own skins. Instead they hid in the underbrush and waited till morning to try again.

At dawn, the other two men rounded up the horses while Simon checked for Indians. He found them, or they found him. Ten mounted Shawnee chased after him. Simon raced into the underbrush and aimed his gun at the leader. Instead of the loud *BOOM* he expected, Simon heard *click, PFFFT*—the rain-dampened powder had misfired. The Shawnee heard it, too, and quickly surrounded him. They dragged him out and bound him to a tree. Bo-nah, their leader, thrust his gun against Simon's chest and kept his finger on the trigger. He had captured the great enemy of the Shawnee tribe and he was taking no chances his enemy might escape.

With a sinking heart, Simon heard a shot from one of the other spies coming to rescue him. After one glance, Simon's rescuer turned and raced away, but he could not outrun the Shawnee bullet sent his way.

Indians enjoy torturing an enemy, so they began to plan how best to teach this white man not to steal their horses. Each man took his turn kicking, beating, and whipping Simon, always taking care not to kill

37

him. Simon steeled himself for worse to come. That night his captors stretched him to the limit and staked him to the ground. Simon spent a painful, sleepless night.

The Shawnee chose an unbroken colt for their prisoner's ride back to Chillicothe. They tied the frontiersman's neck to the horse's neck. They tied his hands behind his back and bound his legs under the colt's belly. The horse bucked and twisted as it raced through the underbrush and tried to scrape Simon off on trees. The Shawnees roared at this sport, but Simon wondered if he would live through it.

At Chillicothe Simon faced running the **gauntlet**. When he saw the double line of Indians with clubs, thorny branches, and poles, he broke out in a cold sweat. If he could reach the council house without falling, he would not have to run a second time. Simon ran for his life, dodging as many of the blows as he could. Four hundred men, women, and children beat Simon's naked body with their weapons, yet he did not fall. But as he staggered to the door of the council house, a sturdy squaw clubbed him to the ground. The Shawnee dragged Simon back for another try.

Simon Kenton Unlikely Hero

The second time he nearly made it, but again went down. The whole crowd circled him and beat and kicked him till he was unconscious.

The Shawnee gave Simon four days of good food and soothing salves so he would recover some strength. They would decide his fate when Chief Black Fish and his men returned after their siege of Boonesborough.

Too soon for Simon, the chief and his war party stormed into the village. The Shawnee had lost thirty-seven men during the siege, so they were in an angry mood. Simon had no hope of being adopted, as Boone had been when he was captured the year before. Instead, they declared him *cut-ta-ho-tha*, or one condemned to die. His death would offset the disgrace of failing to destroy Boonesborough.

The whole tribe must witness this ritual burning of their great enemy. The Shawnee marched their prisoner forty miles to a larger village, Wapatomica. On the way they used Simon's body as a bridge to cross a shallow creek, nearly drowning him. Another time, a squaw threw sand in his eyes, temporarily blinding him. At each village along the way he faced another gauntlet. Even Indians from other tribes came to get a chance to club him. Each time he was beaten till unconscious.

Simon awoke each time to a hearty meal. They even treated his wounds, all to give him strength to run again.

Could he escape? Not at night, since he was stretched and bound to stakes. Nor was escape possible as he marched from village to village with his hands tied behind his back surrounded by armed warriors. Simon plotted to race away when they unbound him before his next gauntlet. When the drums began beating, Simon watched for his moment to bolt for freedom.

Before the starting signal, Simon raced down the line, leapt over a short squaw, and headed for the forest. He heard shouts, but kept running. Knowing he ran for his life gave him extra speed. No Indian could catch this man known for his swiftness. He sprinted for miles, across rocky outcrops and through streams to throw off his pursuers. He had escaped!

At a bend in the trail, Simon stopped dead in his tracks. What he saw made him turn and run the opposite direction. Chief Blue Jacket his men had journeyed to see the famous prisoner's execution. The Shawnee warriors spotted him and urged their horses to the chase. Blue Jacket caught up with Simon, leaned out, and swung his weapon into Simon's skull. Fortunately for Simon, the chief's mighty blow came from the pipe end of his tomahawk.

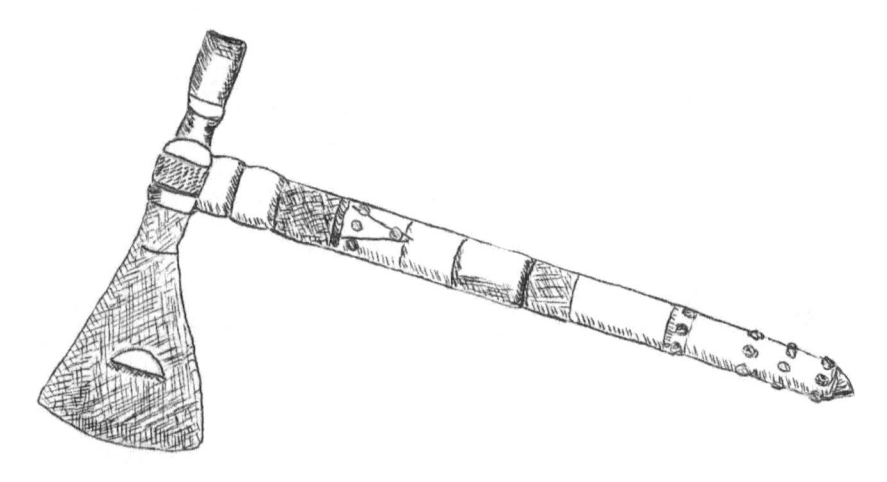

They dragged Simon back, though he remembered nothing for days. For a week his head ached and his thoughts were muddled. He gave up all hope, feeling abandoned by God and man. But the Indians didn't let him die right then; they wanted to watch him die slowly.

At Wapatomica Simon ran the gauntlet again, twice. There the Indians gathered in their fine council house to discuss his fate. Simon had already been declared *cut-ta-ho-tha*, the condemned man. They agreed that in three days, they would slowly roast Simon to death. They painted his face and upper body black.

During those days the squaws and children tormented him with burning sticks, or by slapping and whipping him. But more than the physical agony was the dread of the torture ahead. Simon watched the Indians encircle a tall wooden stake with firewood. He stared this death sentence in the face, knowing it would mean hours of torment. At age twenty-three, he was not ready to die.

As Simon waited for his painful death, a war party returned to Wapatomica with scalps and captives. Who was this condemned man huddled in the council house, naked and blackened for his fate? A member of the war party, Simon Girty, went over to question the captive about the number of fighting men in Kentucky. Girty knew this **intelligence** would be useful to his British superiors at Detroit.

Simon Girty

Simon Girty knew Indian languages and culture. He used this skill as a scout for the Americans. After he was wrongfully jailed, he became a **renegade**, working for the British. He lived among the Shawnee as a British agent. Settlers on the frontier hated Simon Girty. They used to warn their naughty children that Simon Girty would get them!

The blackened prisoner gave evasive answers, so Girty questioned him further. Finally he demanded his name. "Simon Butler," the condemned prisoner answered, and scolded him for not knowing his old friend. Girty was so glad to see his blood brother he threw his arms around him and cried. Girty listened with sympathy as Simon poured out the tale of all his tortures.

Simon Girty had an honored position among the assembled chiefs, so he asked a favor—the life of his friend. Girty reminded them of the prisoner's bravery in the face of all the tortures he had endured so far. The chiefs heard his eloquent speech in silence. Some of the younger chiefs grumbled that they had traveled far to see this man's burning. Yet when the chiefs passed the council club a second time around the circle, only a few struck the ground to vote for death.

These men had seen their prisoner's courage, his skill at running and leaping, and his tricks at outwitting them. Now they crowded around him and congratulated him, calling him brother. A squaw adopted Simon to replace her only son, lost in the recent siege of Boonesborough. She scrubbed Simon to wash away his white skin and gave him a Shawnee name meaning Great White Wolf.

Girty outfitted his friend with horse and saddle, tomahawk and knife, and clothes to fit his large frame. The two Simons roamed the woods together, as in the old days. They traveled to nearby Indian towns—Blue Jacket's Town, McKee's Town, and others. Simon kept a keen eye out for landmarks; someday this knowledge would be valuable. Twenty days of freedom, of healing for Simon, ended with a sudden summons to return to Wapatomica. When they arrived, not one of the Shawnee warriors would shake Simon Butler's hand. Simon's heart sank.

What caused this sudden change? A raiding party had returned from western Virginia after losing half its warriors. They demanded revenge. They argued against reversing a declaration of *cut-ta-ho-tha*. All of Girty's arguments for sparing Simon's life were ignored and the council again voted for his death.

Girty seemed to turn against his friend now. He suggested the execution of such a great enemy as Simon Butler would increase the Shawnee tribe's standing among all the tribes. Thus it should take place at Upper Sandusky, a British trading post fifty miles northeast. Delegations of Wyandot, Cayuga, Chippewa, Potawatomie, Tuscarora, Mingo, and

Delaware would soon assemble there to get their winter allotment of powder and lead.

The Shawnee council approved Girty's new plan. Within the hour Bo-nah and four guards on horseback headed north with Butler staggering behind them, roped by the neck.

Girty galloped in that direction as well, calling to his friend to have courage. Would Girty try to arrange a rescue? Simon's death seemed more certain by the hour.

Girty rode ahead to ask for help from Chief Logan, one who had often aided whites. Logan, a Mingo, admitted his influence with the Shawnee was not great, but said he would do all that he could.

As Simon and his captors stopped for water at a creek, Bo-nah took out his rage for the delayed execution. He smashed his stone war club into Simon's left arm, snapping the bone. Simon's painful journey soon got worse. An old man chopping wood recognized the prisoner. In revenge for his dead son, the man raised his hatchet, aiming to hack off Simon's head. Simon ducked, but the hatchet connected with his right collarbone, breaking it and leaving a deep gash.

With these two terrible injuries, Simon's spirits sank even lower. He could barely drag one foot in front of the other. That night his guards made the pain nearly unbearable by stretching and staking him to prevent his escape.

Simon's spirits rose the second night when they stopped at Chief Logan's winter camp. The two Simons had visited Logan a few weeks before and helped him build a log cabin. Now he treated Simon kindly.

Chief Logan gathered the facts from Bo-nah and the guards and sent two runners to Upper Sandusky to "speak good" for Simon. The chief fed Simon well and splinted the broken arm. Logan invited the guards to hunt with him the next day so the runners would have time to bring back their report.

The runners returned with news for the chief, but Logan kept Simon in the dark about what he had learned. Simon's hopes tumbled. This ominous sign probably meant the chief's efforts could not save him from death at the stake.

The British trading post of Upper Sandusky buzzed with preparations for the long-awaited torture. A tall post stood before the council house and the Indians ringed it with dry firewood. Simon slept little on his final night, knowing at dawn he would be burned.

Early next morning the crowd gathered, ready to light the fire. In the blue sky above him Simon spied one little dark cloud. Suddenly a heavy rain poured down, drenching the firewood, the prisoner, and the whole village. The Indians, always superstitious, wondered if the Great Spirit was protecting the life of the man they intended to kill.

But no, this idea must be wrong. Didn't a second council agree to his fate? Chief Black Hoof declared, "Tomorrow he will die."

The **Providence of God** had intervened to save Simon today, but what would happen tomorrow?

Providence of God

Providence is an old-fashioned word. The settlers understood it to mean God's rule of his universe to bring about his will on earth. They believed in a God who created man and then *provided* for him. To them Providence was "The hand of God inside the glove of human events."

> *Have you ever had a narrow escape from danger? How did it make you feel?*
>
> *What would be your thoughts if you faced certain death?*

7
A Trip to Detroit

November 1778

*S*imon had good reason to believe in the Providence of God. The day of his rescheduled execution brought a British visitor to Upper Sandusky, dressed in a magnificent coat of scarlet and gold. Captain Peter Drouillard came on the very day when Simon Butler was to die. He distributed the annual gifts of powder and lead to the assembled tribes.

This trader and interpreter for the British at Fort Detroit usually wore his trader's garb—moccasins, comfortable leather leggins and a loose blouse. But today he had secret second mission and he needed to impress the Indians. The Indians already knew and respected Drouillard, since he gave them the best prices for their furs. They traded for food, cloth, knives, powder, lead, and rifles. But Drouillard had a difficult task ahead, to convince the Shawnee to give up the pleasure of watching their worst enemy roast to death.

After greeting the chiefs, the trader glanced at the prisoner. Simon, painted black, looked half-dead already. The Shawnee might not allow Drouillard to rescue this poor wretch.

The trader chose his arguments to appeal to the Indians. He told them the English desired that no American be left alive. But their English father in Detroit wanted this man because he could tell them information about the strength of the **long knives.** In fact, an army of Kentuckians was on the way right now to invade Indian villages. The information learned from this prisoner could save the lives of many Shawnee. For their trouble, the trader would give them a hundred dollars' worth of rum, tobacco, salt, gunpowder, or whatever they chose. Bo-nah could even come to Detroit to make sure the prisoner returned.

The trade goods sealed the deal, for the council voted to accept this plan. Soon Drouillard set off for Detroit with Butler, guarded by Bo-nah. Simon felt a bond with this small, dark, and quiet captain who was his God-sent rescuer.

Detroit's neat French farms and relaxed atmosphere contrasted sharply with his previous captivity, like a stroll through the woods differed from a run through the gauntlet.

Commander Hamilton's own doctor worked on Simon's broken arm and other injuries. As he surveyed the patient's many wounds, especially the round dent in his head, the doctor marveled how he had survived.

With a bath, new clothes, and his matted hair shaved off, Butler reported to Detroit's acting commander, Captain Lernault. When questioned about the number of men in the militia, Simon inflated the strength of Kentucky's fighting force. He of all people knew that weakness invites attack.

The captain warned Simon not to try to escape. He gave many good reasons--none have succeeded since we are deep in Indian territory and there is no way to get through to the American settlements. The last reason should have made Simon shudder--any recaptured prisoners are executed. Of course Simon planned to escape, but not in winter.

Simon had free range in Detroit and the surrounding area. He used his time to spy on the strength of Detroit's defenses. The British even allowed him in their military councils. Simon got an earful, once hearing the commander thank the Indians for the scalps they had brought, and encouraging them to go get more. He also heard the disappointing news that General Hamilton (nicknamed "the Hair Buyer" because he paid Indians for scalps) had defeated Clark and retaken Vincennes.

Simon Kenton Unlikely Hero

Most prisoners in Detroit worked to earn their keep and were only required to report for roll call every Sunday. Simon's broken arm earned him light duty, helping at John Edgar's trading post. This job afforded Simon many advantages. He overheard bits of information from British soldiers about the fort under construction on the heights above Detroit. Prisoners from Pennsylvania, Kentucky, and all over the frontier bought goods at the trading post. Simon met two fellow prisoners from Kentucky who were brave enough to plan an escape attempt with him. The three of them stashed extra moccasins, a musket with balls and powder, and dried meat, though spring was still months away.

Working for John Edgar had one more advantage. His wife Rachel had sympathy for the American cause and hinted to Simon what would be the best escape route from Detroit. Simon made friends among the British officers, too. Because of his remarkable skill with a rifle he was invited along on their hunting trips. Everyone seemed to know him; they nicknamed him "the Giant".

In late February Simon heard exciting news—George Rogers Clark had retaken Vincennes from Hamilton. Clark had surprised the fort by a daring winter attack. Now Simon was more eager than ever to share all his military information with this bold commander of Kentucky's militia. Detroit's defenses were weak—Clark could easily capture it. With Detroit's capture, the major British influence would be gone from the west.

In spring, Simon itched to try what other Detroit prisoners had never pulled off. His friends in Detroit, the Edgars and Captain Drouillard,[2] stockpiled more food, ammunition, and moccasins for the escape. One evening in June, Simon and two other Kentuckians collected their hidden supplies and disappeared.

Clark Leads a Surprise Winter Attack on Vincennes.

Karen Meyer

Shawnee Point of View

Among the Shawnee, Bo-nah earned fame for his capture of Simon Butler, the great enemy of his people. They called Simon "the man whose gun is never empty" because he could reload while he ran. Simon's courage in the face of great pain boosted the importance of the prisoner as well as the one who captured him.

In Detroit Bo-nah waited in vain for the British to be done with Simon. The British gave the Shawnee more presents as payment for his trouble. As Bo-nah left without his prisoner, he realized Simon Butler would escape his fate once more.

Shawnee Warriors

Many years later, after the Treaty of Greenville brought peace, Shawnee warriors told and retold the story of how Simon escaped death. They declared the Great Spirit above took him from them a little by little, and then a little farther, and finally took him away altogether. Simon, too, could not shake the feeling his many escapes from death were due to God's Providence.

Would you disobey the law to help a friend in trouble?

8
Home to Kentucky

June 1779 - June 1780

At first Simon and the other two escapees headed *north*west to throw off pursuers. For two weeks they steered by the stars, traveling at night to evade capture. They tramped four hundred miles through swamps and hills, wearing out their moccasins, then their feet. Raccoon cooked over an open fire kept them from starvation. They kept a sharp eye out for Indians, but didn't see a single one during the whole thirty-day trek between Detroit and Fort Vincennes, in Indiana Territory.

Simon rejoiced to be a free man again. When he walked through George Rogers Clark's door, his old friend jumped up and grabbed his hand, saying he'd thought Simon was dead. He listened eagerly to what Simon said about Detroit's weak defenses. He agreed with Simon this prize should be captured, but sadly he didn't have the army to carry it out. Both men were disappointed. They knew this British post would continue to conduct attacks against American settlements and supply Indians with guns and powder.

Leaving Clark, Simon hurried back to Kentucky to surprise his other friends. Instead, a big surprise awaited Simon Butler.

Some newcomers canoeing down the Ohio had stopped for the night and Simon joined them. One man looked familiar, so Simon chatted with him and asked him lots of questions. Imagine Simon's joy when he learned it was John Kenton, his own brother! After hugs and a few tears, John updated his brother on news of their family and neighbors. Simon's jaw dropped when he heard that William Leachman was not dead. In fact, he had been tried for Simon's murder, but acquitted for lack of evidence. Simon had carried the burden of Leachman's murder on his conscience for eight years. Now that burden was gone.

Simon no longer needed to hide behind an alias, so he immediately took his own name back. From that day forward the name Simon Kenton grew in reputation on the frontier. Simon had kept quiet about himself for fear his past would get him into trouble. Now he traded stories with the new settlers he advised and guided.

Land Speculators

Land speculators bought thousands of acres of land in the Ohio Country from the government. They bought at a low price, had surveyors divide it, and hoped to resell the land to settlers for a profit. Some men made their fortunes, but others lost their shirts. If the speculator didn't pay the entire amount to the government by the deadline, he lost the land. Those who bought lots from him also lost their land.

Kentucky had changed while Simon was gone. Everywhere surveyors and **speculators** bought and sold land. Virginia opened a land office in Kentucky County in October of 1779. Simon claimed 400 acres and

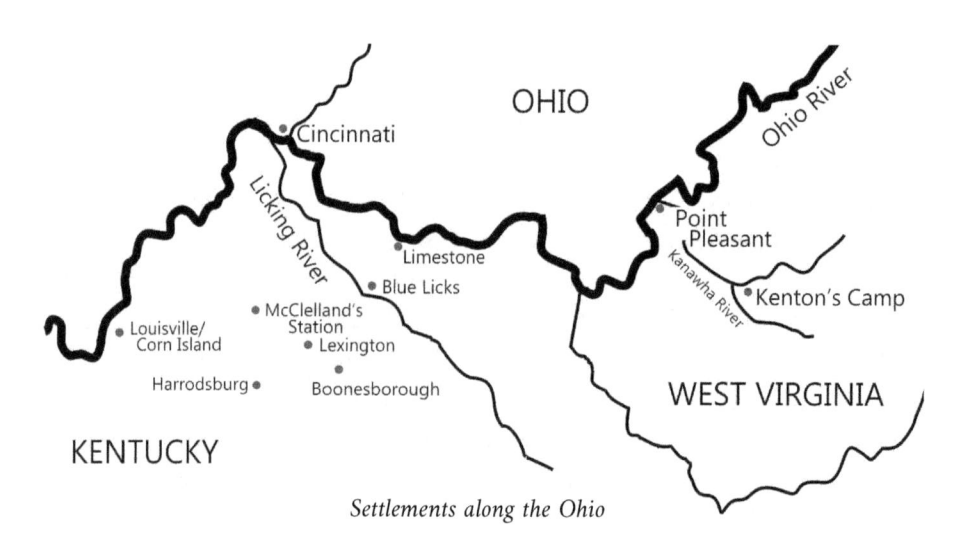

Settlements along the Ohio

Simon Kenton Unlikely Hero

registered it under his own name. The flood of settlers continued, spurred on by the War for Independence still raging in the east and south.

Simon became a **locator** for other settlers buying property. Few others knew this land as well as Kenton. He had roamed far and wide, and he remembered the forests, hills, and streams he had seen. The settlers often paid him in land for his services. His land holdings continued to grow until he owned thousands of acres in Kentucky.

That winter turned cold early and stayed cold till spring. Turkeys froze on their roosts and dropped to the ground. The streams and rivers froze solid. Snow was so deep whole herds of deer starved to death. It was a tough time for the Kentucky settlers, who for years afterward called it the Hard Winter. The only good thing—the Indians did not attack the settlements.

In June, the British dragged Kentucky into the War for Independence. Captain Henry Bird enlisted a horde of Indians from many tribes, more than six hundred warriors. In addition, he commanded a hundred Redcoats and seventy green-coated Canadian Rangers. The two cannons hauled to battle by this impressive army guaranteed their victory. Simon Kenton shuddered. Wooden forts would splinter under the big guns.

Captain Bird's army first attacked Ruddell's Station. *BOOM!* A cannon ball tore apart the corner blockhouse and the station quickly surrendered. Ruddell agreed to Captain Bird's conditions—the men would become British prisoners, and the women and children could find shelter in other forts. But the Indians devised their own plan. They stormed into the fort, scalping helpless settlers until Bird finally shamed them into stopping. The attackers loaded the remaining settlers with booty and herded them like cattle to the next target, Martin's Station.

The other stations could offer little help. Their settlements would be attacked next, so they made what preparations they could. Simon led a small group from Harrodsburg to see the damage at Ruddell's and to bury the dead. There they learned the details of what happened to Bird's second target, Martin's Station. In the face of the cannon and overwhelming force, Martin's also surrendered. At least Bird prevented more scalping.

This second victory put Captain Bird in a difficult position. He was burdened with 450 prisoners, too many to feed. His Indian allies itched to solve the problem by adding more scalps to their belts. Bird did something no one expected—he abandoned the rest of the campaign.

This enraged the Indians, who scorned this British captain. Only a faint-hearted leader would refuse them the pleasure of killing the helpless settlers inside the forts. With the power of the British cannons, they expected to demolish the remaining Kentucky settlements, one by one. The Indians headed home, loading their share of prisoners with booty like packhorses. A smaller group of sixty Indians, determined to continue the victories, attacked and destroyed little Grant's station.

The British army, with their share of prisoners, canoed back across the Ohio. The last canoe and its valuable cannon mysteriously disappeared. Simon and another scout sank the unwieldy craft carrying a **six-pounder**. They carefully marked the spot and later raised it for use in future battles. This tiny victory encouraged the settlers in the face of the grim defeat Captain Bird had inflicted.

The British marched their prisoners to Fort Detroit, a journey of six hundred miles. Husbands and wives and children were often separated, making the hardships they faced even worse. Survivors of the trip could not return home or begin searching for their families until three or four years later, when the war was over. Some of the captive children were adopted by Indians, and didn't return to their families for as long as fifteen years. One of the children adopted into the Shawnee tribe was Stephen Ruddell, the twelve-year-old son of the founder of Ruddell's station. He was adopted into Tecumseh's family and given the name Sinnanatha, or Big Fish. Because they were the same age, the two boys became close friends. They hunted and fished together and taught each other their native tongues. Twelve years later, Tecumseh's band of one hundred Shawnee, including his adopted brother Sinnanatha, returned north from raiding the Kentucky settlements. Simon Kenton, leading the scouting party to recover stolen horses, tracked and attacked the Shawnee camp after midnight. In the clash, Sinnanatha almost shot Kenton, but his gun misfired because of wet powder. The Ruddell family had double sorrow; they not only lost a child, but also had their son fighting against the settler's cause.

How would you react to being a prisoner of the Indians or the British?

9
Clark to the Rescue

August 1780

Kenton and the other Kentuckians were fighting mad. Two settlements had been destroyed and a total of 470 settlers either killed or taken prisoner. Captain Bird had done his evil work and returned to Detroit, hundreds of miles away. Kentuckians focused their fury on the Indians instead. They demanded George Rogers Clark command a Kentucky militia campaign into Indian territory. Simon and his fellow Kentuckians so respected Clark's leadership that one thousand of them joined him to fight.

These rugged woodsmen were set in companies under five colonels. Simon Kenton, now Captain Kenton, commanded a company of scouts. They assembled at the mouth of the Licking River with their horses, boats, provisions, and cannon, ready to cross the Ohio and march against the Shawnee.

From the future site of Cincinnati, Kenton rode ahead to mark the trail for the army. As he drew close to Chillicothe,

Clark's Campaign against the Shawnee

54

he smelled smoke. Simon had seen a deserter slip away the night before, but Clark had forbidden pursuit. Someone, perhaps that deserter, had warned the Shawnee to flee; they had torched the village as they headed north. Now it lay in ashes with some of the cabins still sending plumes of smoke into the morning sky.

The army took time to destroy acres of corn and vegetables. But their main objective was to meet and fight the Shawnee, so they marched north to the next village, Piqua.

On a broad plain in front of the town, the Shawnee clashed with the Kentuckians. When the Indians retreated to their British-built blockhouse, the militia brought up their captured cannon. *BOOM!* The cannonballs found their target and demolished the fortress. The militiamen inflicted revenge for the splintered blockhouses of Martin's Station and Ruddell's Station.

The Indians fell back to a new defensive position, the cliffs and trees behind the town. All afternoon bullets whizzed from both sides in a fierce battle. Simon excelled at this type of combat, with his deadly aim and ability to load on the run. The Kentucky militia outnumbered the Shawnee, so late in the day the Indians disappeared into the woods, carrying their dead comrades. Again the men had to be satisfied cutting down corn and destroying gardens. As they departed, they torched the town.

In less than a month, the army marched home. Colonel Clark was pleased with their work against the Shawnee. He wrote to Thomas Jefferson, Governor of Virginia, "Nothing could excel the . . . Kentuckyans [sic] that compose this little army in bravery and implicit obedience to orders."

These victories, however, had long-term consequences. Because their gardens had been destroyed, the Shawnee had a tough winter. In early spring, they attacked the throngs of newcomers coming downriver loaded with provisions for the frontier. Few survivors escaped this Shawnee method of replenishing their food supplies. Simon ached as he watched wrecked canoes and flatboats float past Limestone on the Ohio. He stepped forward to help when he could and guided newcomers to their land.

They came by the thousands! Harrodsburg and Danville, Stanford and Lexington blossomed into towns. These hardy pioneers wanted to make their own laws instead of being part of Virginia. Eleven years later, in June of 1792, Kentucky wrote its own constitution and became a state.

Kentucky drew settlers like flowers draw bees, and Simon knew why. Kentucky's charms included abundant game, fertile land, and the chance for settlers to claim land of their own. Men and women braved Indian attacks, disease, and hardships to come settle in the wilderness.

Taverns sprang up all over, which Simon disapproved. Drunken Indians committed the worst cruelties. He knew the poison of liquor would eventually destroy a person. Three of Simon's friends—Peter Drouillard, George Rogers Clark, and Chief Logan—all became enslaved by alcohol.

Simon's land holdings continued to grow. Requirements for a claim included slashing boundary trees with his "K" and building a cabin. One of his claims perched beside Lawrence Creek, near the cane lands he had first explored. He considered going back to his parents' farm in Virginia, since it had been nine years since he fled from home. Some day he would bring them here to live in this beautiful land, but he was too busy right now.

Would you trade a safe home in the east for the dangers of a wilderness farm?

10
Revolutionary War Battles

1781 and 1782

Captain Bird's attacks on Kentucky forts brought the war for independence home to Simon and his fellow Kentuckians. For five years, red-coated soldiers had battled colonial armies in Virginia, Pennsylvania, Maryland, New York, New Jersey, and New England. Later, the southern states' militia joined the battles, too.

Now, in the fall of 1781, General George Washington won a stunning victory for the colonies. British General Cornwallis surrendered his entire army at Yorktown, Virginia. The thirteen colonies had finally won their war for independence. But that didn't end the fighting. For two years, various skirmishes pitted British and Indians against the Colonials. The Treaty of Paris in 1783 marked the official end of the war.

On the frontier, settlers and Indians continued attacking each other. In early spring a Pennsylvania militia group of a hundred men was sent to punish the warlike Delaware for their attacks on the settlements. Instead, Colonel David Williamson marched into the Ohio country to attack and kill a group of peaceful Delaware who had converted to Christianity.

A Sad Story: the Moravian Massacre

Frontier warfare forced Indian tribes to choose sides. Many tribes joined forces with the British. A few helped the Americans. The Moravian Christian Delaware Indians tried to remain neutral, but were suspected by both sides of helping their enemy. Reverend David Zeisberger, their leader, settled one group of converts in the village of Gnadenhutten, in Ohio Country.

Colonel David Williamson, leader of Pennsylvania militia, attacked this group of families as they worked in the field. He falsely accused them of raiding towns in Pennsylvania. He promised them food and clothing, but then ordered them bound and locked up in their meetinghouse.

When Williamson told them the militia had voted to put them to death, Abraham, their chief, pleaded for their lives. "I call upon God as my witness that we are innocent of any crime against you." The entire group spent the night in prayer and singing, knowing they would soon see their Savior. The next morning their cruel execution was carried out. Ninety-six men, women, and children died. Two fourteen-year-old boys escaped to warn the other Delaware settlement.

The Indians refused to make peace with such a cold-blooded enemy; they would fight them to the death. Retaliating for the Moravian massacre, the Indians raided with no mercy and took no captives. The Pennsylvania militia, instead of punishing the man who committed the massacre, sent a new leader, Colonel Crawford, to finish the job. This army marched toward the Delaware villages on the Upper Sandusky River.

This time their attack met strong resistance. These were the warlike Delaware, the original targets of the Pennsylvania militia. In the hasty retreat from an Indian force three times as large as his own, Colonel Crawford was captured. The Delaware Indians took out their fury on him for the massacre. One chief told Colonel Crawford, "The blood of the innocent Moravians . . . cruelly and wantonly murdered, calls loudly for revenge." The wretched prisoner was first tortured and then burned at the stake in a slow and painful death. This event sent shudders down the spines of Kentucky settlers. Would they be next?

Simon was stunned when he heard of the massacre of these Moravian Indians. He had killed many Indians in battle, but this deed sickened him. Those on the frontier knew danger and death lurked around the next corner. And Kentuckians told each other gruesome stories of the latest cruelty by Indians. But this, Kenton declared, was a "shocking affair."

Battle of Blue Licks

All during the Revolution, the British had recruited Indian allies for their battles to keep their colonies. Sometimes they sent manpower to the tribes, but always they provided guns and powder. The British goal matched the Indian goal, to force settlers to leave Indian lands. Nearly a year after Cornwallis' defeat, a belated battle pitted Kentuckians against the British and their Indian allies.

Captain Caldwell led a force of fifty British Rangers and two hundred and fifty Indians to attack Bryan's Station. Two men escaped the fort by night with an urgent plea for help.

For two days the men and women in this Kentucky settlement refused to give up. They watched helplessly as the Indians slaughtered their cattle and burned their crops. Captain Caldwell, fearing reinforcements were on the way, retreated to Blue Licks. This lick, a major source of salt, attracted Indians, settlers, and game of all kinds.

Half the militia reinforcements arrived at Bryan's Station and easily followed the attackers' trail the forty-five miles to Blue Licks. Should they strike now or wait for the rest of the militia? Colonel Daniel Boone warned them the ravines could conceal hundreds of enemies, and advised them to wait.

One fierce Indian fighter argued for charging ahead. Hotheaded Captain Hugh McGary shouted, "All who are not cowards, follow me!" After discussing strategy, the one hundred eighty men did follow, straight into the ambush set for them by the British and Indians.

Seventy of Kentucky's best men died that day, (August 19, 1782) including Daniel Boone's son Israel. Simon arrived early the next day with the reinforcements. Too late to help fight, their sad task was to bury the dead.

In the fall of 1782, when the Indians heard about Cornwallis' defeat, their attacks in Kentucky increased. They fought hard, knowing this might be their last chance to drive the white settlers from their lands.

Even after the Treaty of Paris officially ended the War for Independence, Simon could not relax his watchfulness. Britain still kept forts on American land. Indians still wanted to push the settlers back across the mountains. Kentucky settlements were still in danger.

Simon and other Kentuckians appealed to George Rogers Clark to lead the militia against the Indians again. As he had two years before, Clark gathered a thousand-man army at the mouth of the Licking River. They left on November 1, hauling along the same six-pound cannon Simon had captured.

Simon Kenton, in the role he enjoyed, piloted the army into Indian country along the same route they used two years ago. Trips to the Shawnee villages brought back memories of his Indian captivity four years before. Simon's body still showed the marks of his tortures—the dent in his head and the stripes on his back. The bones that were broken ached whenever the weather changed. Despite the painful memories, Simon again admired the scenery around him. He determined to claim land in Ohio someday.

Most of the Indian towns gave them little or no resistance. The soldiers burned the towns and destroyed all stores of food. Indian snipers took shots at them and grazed the arm of one man fighting beside Kenton. Captain Victor McCracken did not expect to die from his painful wound, but gangrene set in as they rode back to the Ohio. When they reached the mouth of the Licking River, the dying captain looked at the lovely Kentucky country around him. Seven short years before, this land had been wilderness. Now twenty thousand settlers called Kentucky home. Captain McCracken mused on the many who had fought and died to win this land. He had a vision of what the future years would bring.

At the captain's funeral, Colonel Clark shared that vision of Kentucky's future with the thousand men drawn up in formation. He suggested a reunion of this brave army in fifty years. Simon and the others agreed to meet then in Newport, Kentucky. None of them knew what the future years would bring, or even if they would be alive to attend.

Can you imagine what a fifty year-reunion with your friends would be like?

11
Simon's Homecoming

1783

Simon wondered whether his parents, brothers, and sisters were thriving back in Virginia. In the spring of 1783, twenty-eight-year-old Simon Kenton headed up the Ohio back to his birthplace to bring his family to Kentucky, the land he loved. On the way upriver, he saw hundreds of canoes and flatboats floating downriver, bringing more settlers to Kentucky.

Memories came flooding back as Simon tramped past the cornfields he had once refused to hoe. Approaching his homestead, he fretted at fences falling down, weeds in the garden, and shingles sliding off the cabin roof. He knocked at the door and his mother slowly opened it.

Flatboats on the Ohio

Mary Kenton had no idea why this big stranger stood on her doorstep. But wait . . . she knew that voice! Simon, her long-lost son hugged her as tears rolled down her cheeks. She hugged and kissed him, trying to make up for the twelve years he had been gone.

Simon's father Mark, feeble and in poor health, perked up when he saw his son. Next day, neighbors flocked around the porch to catch Simon's stories. Simon had plenty of yarns to tell, and he enjoyed telling them. We can imagine the hairs on the back of their necks tingling as Simon recounted his narrow escapes, his rescues of captured settlers, and his exploits against the Indians with Daniel Boone and George Rogers Clark.

Simon called the Kenton clan together to convince his brothers and sisters of the wonders and benefits of Kentucky. Simon owned so much land he offered every family member two hundred fifty prime acres. The tiny leased farms of Virginia looked like garden plots in comparison. He also promised a hundred acres to any Virginia neighbors who came to Kentucky.

Mark and Mary Kenton caught Simon's enthusiasm and started packing what they would need. Their list included their big loom, spinning wheels for both wool and flax, scythes, rakes, hoes, forks, corn for seed, mallets, axes, a big kettle for soap-making, cooking pots, a churn, pottery, clothes, featherbeds, blankets, the family Bible, and *Pilgrim's Progress*. The

Conestoga Wagon

Simon Kenton Unlikely Hero

animals went along to Kentucky, too—chickens, geese, dogs, a sow, a horse, and a **heifer**.[3] The Kentons said goodbye to neighbors and to the simple log cabin, built with Mark's own hands.

Simon hired a big **Conestoga wagon** with driver and team to haul his parents and their goods over the mountains. Forty people, including relatives and neighbors, gathered to form a caravan. The wagons lumbered up and down hills in the August heat. They aimed to reach Redstone Old Fort on the Monongahela River where they would have a flatboat built to order. Then the Ohio River would be their highway.

Simon's elderly father Mark knew he might not survive the journey, but he declared he'd go as far as he could. He longed for a better life for his children and grandchildren. His own life had been spent scratching out a meager living on a tenant farm. As the wagon jolted over every bump on the trail, Simon's father lost his frail hold on life. He would never see that Promised Land his son had so vividly described. The family held his simple burial service beside the Monongahela River.

Simon ordered a Kentucky-style flatboat for their group. The clumsy craft measured thirty-five feet wide and fifty feet long. The cabin on one end sheltered the forty passengers, their goods, and a cooking area. The stock pen sported high walls to protect the animals from Indian attack. On the crowded but pleasant flatboat ride, Simon pointed out sights along the way. They passed Point Pleasant, the memorable spot where Chief Cornstalk's army of Indians fought a valiant battle in Lord Dunmore's War. Every day the boat stopped to get firewood and to let Simon hunt. He never failed to bring them dinner—turkey, deer, and once a small bear.

The first day of November they arrived at Limestone, their goal. Simon's heart warmed to see his home settlement again. He had planned to stay, but signs of Indians were everywhere--hidden canoes, moccasin tracks. Simon guided his family and the others inland to his old settlement on Quick's Run. A November wind whistled through the cracks between the logs of the four dirt-floored cabins. Simon convinced the group that safety was more important than comfort right now. He

63

Karen Meyer

worked hard, chinking the cracks between the logs to make the temporary quarters livable for his mother. She and the others shivered and remembered their snug Virginia cabins.

What would tempt you to leave your familiar home to travel to a new place?

12
Building Kenton's Station

1784 and 1785

*S*imon returned in the spring to Limestone settlement to welcome the crowds of settlers landing there. Many stayed, attracted by the site's wide landing and the buffalo road to the interior. This place would soon have enough men for a **station**. Simon claimed more land in the area, slashing his K into the trees at the corner of each claim.

On the last day of 1784, a group of small boats arrived at Limestone landing. William Wood, a Baptist preacher, and two other families had traveled down the Ohio, hoping to settle in Louisville, Kentucky. Ice on the river made further travel dangerous, so they landed at Limestone.

Simon Kenton welcomed them; the settlers needed a preacher. They longed to have church services like they had back home. Later Simon's two brothers and a delegation from the three tiny communities nearby urged the group to stay. Simon offered to sell them "land as good and as cheap" as anywhere else in Kentucky. William Wood and his friends caught Simon's enthusiasm as he showed them the cane fields, the rolling hills, and the clear springs.

The property pleased them so much they bought four hundred acres. They **platted** a town and named it Washington to honor the general who won the nation's independence.

Simon was delighted to see Kenton's Station growing. It mushroomed the following year when twenty families arrived and built cabins facing each other, joined in a square. In each corner stood a two-story **blockhouse** for protection against Indian attack. On one side of the square a tall picket wall ran between two cabins. Each cabin door, three inches thick, was barred at night for safety.

That fall, a budding young author arrived in the nearby settlement of Washington. Sixteen-year-old James Finley admired Simon Kenton and the two became friends. James taught Simon how to write his own name so he no longer had to use an X to sign documents. Young Finley kept a journal of happenings on the Kentucky frontier. Through his journal we glimpse Simon Kenton through another's eyes.

Finley's entry for October 31, 1785: "Today we finished the O'Bannon cabin. That's 31 cabins here in Washington now not counting the one where Reverend Wood does his preaching. Getting to be a regular town for sure! Even got a wagon road through the cane alls [sic] the way into Limestone. Mr. Kenton kept a lookout for danger whilst we worked. He is a truly great adventurer. He is truly the master spirit in this region and he means a lot to us here. Everybody here looks on him as the great defender, always on the alert, and ready to fly at a moments notice to a place of danger for the protection of the scattered familys [sic] in this wilderness. He is the teacher and captain of all the young boys in these parts and I regard him as the prince of pioneers of this region of the country. Pa says he considers him as a man raised up by **Providence** for a special purpose because of the miraculus [sic] way he was delivered up from perils and he says he is for certain a Child of Providence."

Simon Kenton Unlikely Hero

What a change from Simon Kenton the brawler who hated to do his chores! Now, as a role model for young boys, he puts himself in danger to protect the settlement.

Simon Kenton enlisted in the militia with the rank of Major. Unofficially, Simon raised his own unpaid army of about forty spies and scouts. This group of "Kenton's boys" awaited a word from Simon to go anywhere he said. At the first sign of an emergency they dropped whatever they were doing and charged out to rescue kidnapped settlers or reclaim stolen horses from the Indians. Many of these men later used their leadership skills to serve their country. One of Kenton's boys, Joseph Vance, became an early governor of Kentucky.

Simon built a fine brick house on a hill overlooking Kenton's Station. His home was a place of hospitality for friends and strangers alike.[4] Simon welcomed visitors with "Take seats, take seats, I'm right glad to see ye." As the visitors had their simple meal of pork and **hominy**, they would trade stories with their host. Simon's soft voice in his old Irish/English dialect would begin, "Well, I'll tell ye . . ." He often related the story of his capture by Shawnee and his escape from burning at the stake.

Simon loved this land. He had family near by, friends who respected him, and a chance serve fellow settlers using his scouting skills. Simon's tenant farmers kept his **corncribs** full and he never refused to share with travelers and with the poor.

Simon Kenton at thirty-three years of age had never married. A bride would make his life complete. But any woman who married this rugged frontiersman must know how to endure hardships. The young lady who won Simon's heart had lived in frontier Kentucky and didn't expect a soft life. Martha "Patsey" Dowden was a distant relation, through Simon's brother's wife.

That first wedding in Kenton's Station took place in February of 1787. Frontier folk gathered from all the nearby settlements to enjoy the traditional big feast and all-night dance after the ceremony. Preacher Wood asked Simon the time-honored question, "Do you, Simon Kenton, take this woman, Martha Dowden, to be your lawfully wedded wife, to love and to cherish, in joy and in sorrow, in sickness and in health, till death do you part?" Simon, who daily braved dangers, might have been nervous as he took this big step in life.

The following years were happy years for Simon and Martha. They welcomed their first child, Nancy, in November of 1787.[5] In 1790, their first son, John, was born. In 1793, Simon's eighty-two-year-old mother arrived by wagon from a nearby settlement to help with the birth of their third child. Frontier babies were born at home with older women acting as midwives. In the early morning hours, Mary Kenton helped in the delivery of a husky baby boy. This baby had a mop of auburn hair just like baby Simon's hair thirty-eight years before. Simon agreed; he named his son Simon Kenton, Junior.

Simon didn't change his ways after he married. Always restless, he often disappeared without notice for days or weeks. Besides riding to help rescue settlers from Indian raids, he might be claiming more land, or checking on his general stores. Simon loved children, but sometimes he found more important things to do than paying attention to his own offspring. More than once he was off on a trip when the newest child joined the family. With baby Sarah's birth in 1795, the Kentons had four children.

Martha waited and watched for Simon to return from each dangerous scouting trip. Would her husband, the father of their children, make it home safely? Life on the frontier had no guarantees; death often came suddenly and unexpectedly. Indians attacked. Diseases—like cholera, typhoid, and smallpox—took their toll as well.

In 1796, death snatched two from the Kenton household. Neither disease nor Indian attack caused this unexpected tragedy. Martha napped as the delivery of their fifth child neared. A fire in the room above burned through the ceiling and collapsed it over her bed, trapping her under burning embers. She was severely burned. She gave birth to a stillborn child and died from her injuries soon afterward.

Some people turn to their faith after losing a loved one, but Simon did not have this comfort. He held his grief inside, taking no interest in helping family and friends repair his brick house. Leaving his in-laws to care for the children, Simon took his rifle, knife, and land-measuring

Simon Kenton Unlikely Hero

chain and hiked for miles through the wilderness. There he could give way to his grief with tears and with shouts that echoed back from the hills. He soaked in the beauty of the trees, streams, and valleys. He slashed his mark to claim more land. The wilderness healed his sorrow and restored the old Simon Kenton.

Have you ever had to face a big problem or sorrow in your life? How did you handle it?

13
From Wilderness to Settled Land

1787-1791

*S*imon Kenton changed Kentucky's northern frontier from a wilderness to a land of farms and settlements. In 1785, Kentucky's population numbered about twenty thousand. With Simon and his trained scouts patrolling the river, more and more settlers braved the many dangers of the frontier. In five years Kentucky's population grew to over seventy thousand.

In 1787, the same year Simon and Martha were married, the federal government established the Northwest Territory. All the land to the north and west of the Ohio River and north to the Canadian border was organized into a **commonwealth.** The charter of this new territory recognized every man as free and equal; no slavery was

Northwest Territory Showing Current State Boundaries

70

permitted. The charter also encouraged both religion and education. This territory later became five states: Ohio, Michigan, Indiana, Illinois, and Wisconsin, and part of Minnesota.

Land speculators bought huge chunks of the Ohio country. Teams of surveyors risked their scalps to mark it into sections. Simon bought a quarter of a million acres in Ohio from one of the biggest land speculators, John Cleves Symmes. Rufus Putnam's Ohio Company founded Marietta, the first permanent settlement in the Northwest Territory. Settlers flooded into Ohio country making the Indians even more determined to drive them back.

In Kentucky, attacks increased and settlers lived in fear. Again and again Simon and his team of young men raced to rescue kidnapped settlers or reclaim stolen horses. One of these rescues, in 1790, highlights Kenton's skills as a scout and woodsman.

Seventeen-year-old James Livingston had run away from home to seek his fortune. He drove a team of horses hauling wagonloads of food supplies for the militia. As he and two other drivers jolted along the rutted road to Limestone, Indians attacked all three wagons. They killed the other two drivers and captured Livingston. After destroying the supplies, they headed back toward the Ohio River with the horses and their prisoner.

Kenton got word of the young man's capture and set out with a party of rescuers on horseback the next morning. Simon and his boys found the Indians' trail and followed it across the Ohio. Next day, after half a day's travel, they spotted the Indians, who bolted away with their prisoner. The rescuers followed the trail, but stopped. The Indians had split into three groups to make tracking more difficult.

Which trail should they follow? Kenton scouted each one, and then chose the middle trail. They followed this trail for two miles, but then it forked again into two trails. Kenton again scouted down each one, and chose one to follow. Would this trail lead them to Livingston? They tracked the group until twilight and camped for the night. Sneaking close to them at daylight, Kenton and his boys heard the sounds of Indians breaking camp, so they followed.

Far ahead, five figures on foot led a horse loaded with skins. Livingston might be in the group, but the distance made it impossible to tell. The rescuers shot one Indian, three men ran away, and one man turned and shouted, "Wagon, my wagon!" Livingston had been dressed like an Indian, but called a signal to Kenton and his boys. After his rescue he pranced around the camp, weeping and laughing with joy.

How did Simon Kenton choose the right trail after the Indians split up twice? He had been tracking and scouting since he left home nearly twenty years before. Tiny clues others might miss gave him a sixth sense for making the right decisions. His skill delivered many settlers who had been captured by Indians.

Simon and his scouts could barely keep up with the calls for help as Indian raids increased to one or more a week. Settlers begged the Kentucky militia to attack the Indians. They needed a new leader, since the militiamen had lost confidence in George Rogers Clark's ability. Those who accused him of getting drunk while on duty forced him to resign.

When Simon visited him, Clark ranted over the neglect and stupidity of an ungrateful country. Simon noticed that he used alcohol to forget the debts the nation owed him.

In August of 1791, General Arthur St. Clair led an army to fight the Indians. St. Clair, the new governor of the Northwest Territory, determined to end the Indian attacks. He planned either to destroy the Indians or force them to surrender. Simon refused to join this campaign. Simon Girty[6] fought alongside the Indians and Kenton never wanted to meet his blood brother in battle. Instead, Kenton continued running his patrols of the Ohio River, guarding against Indian raids.

St. Clair marched 1,300 mostly untrained militiamen northward, building forts along the way. Chief Little Turtle's spies stalked them, reporting every move they made. St. Clair's army was shocked awake at dawn as 1,500 Indians swooped down on their camp. Every man ran for his life, leaving the wounded behind. The general lost half his men and all his supplies. St. Clair's expedition holds the record for "the worst defeat ever to be suffered by an American army at the hands of Indians."[7]

Simon Kenton Unlikely Hero

After their decisive victory, the Indians renewed their fierce raids against the settlements. Their way of life would disappear if the settlers continued to flood into Ohio. They determined to drive the whites from the Ohio country. Many settlers pulled up stakes and traveled back across the Allegheny Mountains. Land values on both sides of the Ohio River dropped.

Simon Kenton refused to surrender in this battle between two ways of life. He loved Kentucky and his thriving station, so he defended the Kentucky settlements with all the skills he had learned in his short lifetime.

Your future will bring some challenges, too. Will you meet those challenges with determination to win? Or will you give up at the first defeat?

14
The Greenville Treaty

1794 and 1795

*S*imon Kenton and the rest of the Kentucky settlers celebrated the choice of Major General "Mad Anthony" Wayne to lead the next expedition against the Indians. Simon appreciated the reputation of this general—a fighter with many battles to his credit. Wayne admired Simon's skills, too. He appointed Kenton a Major in the militia and let him choose a hundred volunteer scouts.

General Wayne determined not to repeat the shameful defeats of the previous two Indian campaigns. He recruited 2,500 regulars and 1,000 volunteers and drilled his men at Cincinnati before heading north. Next he built forts—Fort Recovery and the larger Fort Greenville for his winter quarters. But Simon and his crew of one hundred scouts (and nine friendly Indians) were restless and eager for battle. They rode out on raids and captured prisoners for questioning.

Even as General Wayne prepared for war he sent peace messengers to the tribes. He gave the Seven Indian nations a choice—peace or total destruction. The Indians' answer? No! Hadn't they soundly defeated the last two American armies that came against them? But Chief Little Turtle warned the Indian leaders about *this* chief. General Wayne never slept and was never surprised at Indian attacks. But the Indians still refused peace talks because of one main point of difference—the Americans insisted on their claim to the Northwest Territory.

Before any real battles began, **swamp fever**[8] laid Kenton so low he could barely walk. He raged at his weakness, but the fever kept recurring and he could not lead his scouts. At one point the fever brought him close to death. He was discharged from the army, went back home, and followed the reports of the army's progress.

Simon and all Kentucky rejoiced at the news of General Wayne's victory over the Seven Nations under Chief Blue Jacket. The final battle, the Battle of Fallen Timbers, proved to the Indians that the British would not help them when they needed it most. Now the tribes begged for peace.

Simon rode to Fort Greenville in 1795 to observe the treaty negotiations. Many treaties had been signed over the years between the settlers and the Indians. One side or the other broke them, often before the year was out. General Wayne wanted this treaty to end all treaties. He invited all twelve tribes[9] of the Northwest Territory to meet at Fort Greenville. He certified each representative as one approved to speak for the tribe.

Groups of Indians arrived over a period of two months, dressed in their finest ceremonial costumes. Over a thousand Indians gathered around the council fires to negotiate. Both sides gave long speeches and exchanged beaded **wampum belts**. These elaborately woven bands recorded the important points of the speech using symbols and colors.[10]

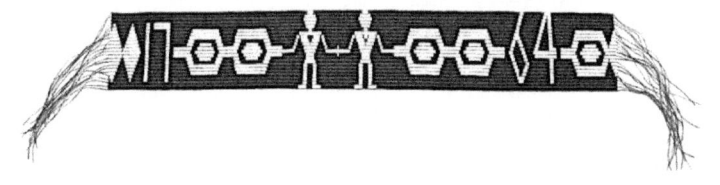

General Wayne welcomed the Indians with flowery words to match their own. "The ground on which this council house stands is unstained with blood and is as pure as the heart of General Washington, the great chief of America, and of his great council; as pure as my heart which now wishes for nothing so much as peace and brotherly love."

A few tribal leaders were strongly opposed to the treaty.[11] Some chiefs—Blue Jacket, Black Snake, and Little Turtle—agreed to sign because they had no other choice. After all twelve tribes signed the treaty, Wayne appointed Chief Tarhe of the Wyandots keeper of the official copy for the Indians.

General Wayne sealed the treaty with a farewell address. "I now fervently pray to the Great Spirit that the peace now established may be permanent . . . that your children may learn to cultivate the earth and enjoy the fruits of peace and industry."

Simon and the other Kentuckians wished for peace, too, after years of living in fear. But the great Shawnee Chief Tecumseh had refused to join the large band of Shawnee at Fort Greenville for the treaty signing. For Simon, this cast an ominous shadow over the future.

15

Simon, Landowner in Two States

1797-1802

*S*imon owned thousands of acres of land. His friends called him land-crazy. He didn't care for riches, but he loved adding more land to his holdings. In 1797, Simon claimed and registered **warrants** for 27,000 acres. Simon also bought land from **speculators**. He surveyed land for others and earned more land as his fee. Simon's excellent memory for the streams, hills, and trees of Kentucky made him in demand as a witness in the courts. He spent many hours in court because of battles over land. So many claims overlapped, even the courts couldn't determine the rightful owner.

Simon later lost much of his land. He didn't always make the final payments and sometimes failed to build a cabin as proof of ownership. He also gave away land to friends and family. Sometimes these gifted lands overlapped the borders of another's land and Simon ended up in court.

Simon courted a young lady and asked her to become the second Mrs. Kenton. She even had the same dark hair and blue eyes of the first Mrs. Kenton, her cousin. In March of 1798, Simon married Elizabeth "Betsy" Jarboe, a lovely, educated lady. They left Simon's four children in the care of relatives and went on their honeymoon.

Simon chose the destination for their honeymoon trip—the wilderness that later became Missouri.[12] Of course Simon kept his eyes open for more land to claim. The couple traveled by packhorse and raft, camping out along the way. The new Mrs. Kenton proved herself as rugged as the previous one.

Kentucky had been Simon's home for twenty-eight years. Its 221,000 residents no longer lived in terror of Indian attack. Simon no longer needed to guide and protect new settlers. Speculators crowded the settlements. Daniel Boone, Simon's close friend, had already left Kentucky for the unsettled frontier on the western side of the Mississippi.

Simon and Betsy heard the enticing call of a new frontier, too—not Missouri but Ohio. Simon hoped to leave behind his many legal battles in Kentucky courts over land titles. Ohio had land to be claimed, and Simon hankered to explore and claim some for his own. In 1799, Simon sold much of the land he owned around Kenton's Station and Washington. With Betsy and the children, Simon headed north. A crowd of relatives and friends packed up their belongings and came along with him.

What adventures and trials would their life in Ohio bring? At forty-four years of age Simon was no longer a young man, but this new frontier energized him.

Simon and Betsy lived for a time in the bustling city of Cincinnati, where their first child Matilda was born. In April, Simon led his group by packhorse to the Mad River Valley. Simon owned land there, purchased from big-time land dealer, John Cleves Symmes.

Along the way, Indians greeted Simon as *Cut-ta-ho-tha*, the Condemned Man. Many Indians still called Ohio home. Under the Greenville Treaty, signed four years before, Indians could camp and hunt anywhere in the state.

The Mad River Valley brought memories flooding back for Simon. There he had sprinted between rows of Indians in the gauntlet. Several groups of Indians camped near Simon's new station. Bo-nah, Simon's Shawnee captor, hinted Simon should give him gifts and special treatment. Bon-ah argued he hadn't killed Simon when he had the chance. Two other Indians, Coonahaw and Chiuxca, settled on Simon's land with their families. As Simon's firm friends, they depended on his protection. What a turnabout from his Kentucky days—now Simon protected Indians from whites.

Simon Kenton Unlikely Hero

The large Indian camps in the neighborhood made most settlers fearful, and not without reason. Sometimes drunken tribesmen stole things, even beating or stabbing settlers. People still ran to Simon for help when Indian trouble arose, and he didn't disappoint them. He would visit the Indian camp, interview the ones involved, and act as a mediator in the dispute. The Indians trusted Simon to treat them fairly and so did the settlers. The militia showed their appreciation by electing him Brigadier General.

Near the fourteen cabins and blockhouse of Kenton's new settlement, a new town sprang up. Betsy was invited to name it. She suggested Springfield because of the many springs. This thriving Ohio city now has a population of 60,000 people.

Betsy Kenton was described as "pleasant, well-informed, capable . . . [with] good looks and charming manner." Simon depended on her to do all his reading and writing. The young Kenton children[13] attended the school established at the Mad River settlement in 1801. Simon paid the yearly school fee for his children and the Indian children in the area. He realized the importance of learning to read and write and "do sums."

Simon kept many **irons in the fire**. He traveled to the Missouri territory to set up two general stores, run by his son and his son-in-law. What stock did these stores carry? The following list reveals what pioneers needed or wanted on the frontier. "Corn, whiskey, tobacco, knives, needles, threads, garters, leggins, moccasins, **vermilion**, kegs, lead, powder, paints, blankets, white goods, flour, meal, pork, flints, knife handles, gun screws, scarlet leggins, shirts, leggins for chiefs, and black and white wampum, with a total value of $18,000."

Simon labored to overcome the handicap of being illiterate, unable to read and write. Do you recognize your weaknesses and work to overcome them?

16
Tecumseh

1802-1809

Simon and family were part of the flood of settlers to Ohio, the new frontier. The Greenville Treaty of 1795 brought peace between the twelve Indian tribes of the Northwest Territory and the settlers. It also opened two-thirds of Ohio to settlement. In 1803 Ohio became the 17th state in the union. However, Simon glimpsed trouble on the horizon.

Simon's experience with Indians warned him something was brewing. He knew how they made decisions in their councils. Twice he had met the young Shawnee Tecumseh in battle and saw his skillful leadership. Now Simon was convinced Tecumseh planned to unite all the Indian tribes to fight to win back the Indian lands.

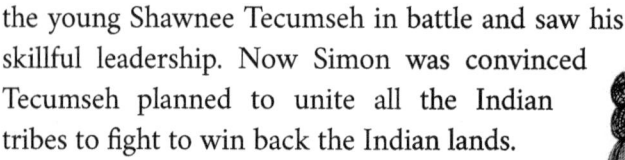

Tecumseh's influence grew as he visited many other tribes and stirred a desire to recover their land from the white man. In 1806, Tecumseh's federation of tribes gathered in one place under the leadership of Tecumseh's brother, the Prophet. The Prophet, using magic tricks to impress his superstitious followers, preached they should give up the white man's ways.

Simon Kenton Unlikely Hero

Rumors flew and fears grew that the Indians planned to attack the settlers. Simon and two other militiamen rode to Chillicothe to find answers. Were the Indians planning war? Simon noticed suspicious signs during the visit, but the Indians denied any plans for battle.

In 1807, unsettling events increased war worries. First, a British **man-of-war** fired on a United States **frigate** and seized four of the sailors. Second, hundreds of Indians gathered at Greenville, and again Kenton went to investigate. He estimated 1,300 warriors in the crowd, most coming from many miles away. More disturbing, they carried new rifles supplied by the British. The Indians refused to shake hands with their right hand, but offered their left hand to Simon and the three men with him. This signaled the Indians were plotting something, perhaps something big.

Simon and the rest of the Ohio settlers were relieved when Tecumseh and his brother moved their horde of followers to Indiana Territory. Prophetstown, on Tippecanoe Creek, gave the Indians an excellent military position. The Prophet began to magnify his own importance to his followers. He announced the prophecies he received from Tecumseh as his own.

How did Tecumseh convince the far-flung tribes to join him? He rode thousands of miles to persuade the leaders of these tribes. He spoke eloquently of the injuries whites had inflicted on the Indians.[14] He also spoke of the great sign that would come to unite all the tribes.

In 1809, Tecumseh gave each partner tribe a post with carved pictograms. Reading from the bottom to the top, the symbols told the tribes to watch for the great sign, a trembling of the earth. When the sign came, all tribes should immediately join Tecumseh and bring their weapons. Runners delivered these carved posts to the thirty major tribes of the west, northwest, north, northeast, and east. Tecumseh himself delivered the posts to the twenty southern tribes. Each tribe also received a bundle of sticks, each stick representing a month. The watching and waiting for Tecumseh's great sign now began.

Karen Meyer

Most Indian tribes fought the settlers, fearing loss of their way of life. A few tribes moved far away. A few tried to stay neutral. What do you think would have been the best way for Indians and settlers to resolve their differences?

17
Simon on the Move

1805

In 1805 Kenton lost his twenty-five thousand acres of Ohio land. It reverted to the government because land speculator John Cleves Symmes could not meet the payments for his two million acre purchase. Kenton had paid Symmes and he could have bought it again from the government, but he refused to pay twice for the same land. Instead, he moved his family near Urbana, where he also owned land. Ten other families joined the Kentons in the little community he called Lagonda (Indian for Horn of the Buck).

Louisiana Purchase Showing Current State Boundaries

Simon didn't let this big setback bother him. His plans kept him traveling. To make travel easier, Simon marked a trail through the wilderness, called a **trace**.[15] Kenton's Trace connected the Mad River Valley to the Ohio River across from Limestone.

Gristmills

As a settlement grew, so did the demand for a gristmill to grind grain into flour. The mill sat beside a waterfall or running stream that turned a water wheel to provide power. The miller first funneled whole grains into the top millstone through a hole in its center. A series of groaning and clanking wooden gears turned the upper millstone. Only the top stone turned, never touching the lower one as it ground the grain. The flour worked its way to the outside of the stationary lower stone through grooves in the stone. Farmers paid a portion of their grain to the miller as his fee for grinding.

Simon had a mill built for him and hired a miller to run it. Farmers needed their corn ground into meal, so the mill prospered. Simon opened a general store and hired someone to run that, too. However, the dishonest manager disappeared, laughing as he pocketed Simon's money.

In 1805, President Thomas Jefferson bought 828,000 square miles of land from France. With the Louisiana Purchase, the nation doubled in size and its frontier advanced west. Simon caught the excitement of new lands to explore. He trekked there with his son John, age 15. He visited his old friend Daniel Boone in Missouri[16] and carried a heavy purse to buy some of these lands for himself.

Simon's land dealings caused him many problems. When Simon sold properties in Kentucky, he guaranteed the title to be clear against all claims. Due to poor surveying some claims overlapped. When the buyers lost their lands, they demanded their money back. One man unjustly claimed

Simon Kenton Unlikely Hero

Simon owed him money, so Kenton refused to pay. The man sued Simon in court and won. Simon was arrested and sent to jail for debt.

The town of Urbana, where the jail was located, loved and respected Simon. The townspeople came up with a solution to help Simon while still obeying the debtor's law. Urbana elected Simon to be his own jailer. He lived in the county jail in six comfortable rooms with his family. He was allowed the freedom to walk from one end of town to the other, so he marched out every day, staff in hand.

During this time, one of his daughters died, eight-year-old Elizabeth. Her funeral was held in the jailhouse parlor, so Simon attended. He trudged as far as the edge of town with the other mourners and stopped. He refused to break his word by going past the town limits to the graveyard. He watched the procession disappear in the distance and sat down on a stone and cried. He comforted himself with a Bible verse, "The Lord giveth and the Lord taketh away." When the Lord gave them another baby daughter some months later, the Kentons named her Elizabeth.

How did Simon perform as a jailer? He took care of prisoners' needs, feeding and providing blankets for them. Most of them found it easy to escape. However, when thieves stole horses from the townspeople, Kenton went into action. He hired three Indians to capture the two men. Simon jailed the thieves to await their trial. They liked to sing and performed requests from others in the jail. One evening, they sang for a long time. When one more request was called out, all was silent. The singing robbers had escaped and dodged justice. At least those two horse thieves never troubled Urbana again.

After Simon spent a year in jail, his friends paid off his debt. Now he was a free man, so he moved his large family to a primitive cabin at the edge of town. This dirt-floored place in Urbana contrasted sharply with his brick home at Kenton's Station. One room had a hollow stump left standing in the center, perfect for pounding hominy. Simon counted this as an advantage, since hominy was his favorite food. Between the two rooms, a roofed porch could be pressed into service for sheltering the many guests who stopped by.

Karen Meyer

Groups of Indians traveled through every six months and camped north of Urbana. They visited the Kentons, and Simon traded with them for moccasins, skins of deer, bear, and wolf, cranberries and other dried fruits, cakes of maple sugar, and honey. He traded items left from his general stores, such as blankets, handkerchiefs, **vermilion**, powder, and lead.

Would you go to jail for something you believed in?

18
Simon at Camp Meeting

1808

In Kentucky, Simon and his family had attended Rev. William Wood's church in nearby Washington. Now in Ohio, they joined the crowds thronging the popular camp meetings. These meetings were part of a spiritual movement called the Second Great Awakening, which began in America in 1790.

Just as the Indians gathered to hear the Prophet preach, settlers gathered to hear preaching as well. Families packed the children and supplies into their wagons and planned for a long stay at the campground. They listened to powerful sermons by Baptist and Methodist preachers.

Camp Meeting, Outdoor Preaching

In 1808 the Kentons again joined the crowds at Voss's campground, near their home. The outdoor preaching from stumps, platforms, and hills brought conviction of sin to Simon's family. Betsy, always the one more interested in such things than Simon, felt God's hand upon her and was converted. Simon, too, pondered much about eternal things. He had killed many Indians in his lifetime. How would he explain his past to God at Judgment Day? This question troubled him and he could not rest. Simon asked one of the preachers to stroll in the woods with him.

When they were far from the crowds, Simon declared he would reveal something to the preacher, but for his ears alone. When he had the promise of secrecy, Simon confessed what a great sinner he had been, and how merciful God had been to preserve him through the dangers of the wilderness. Simon wept and the preacher wept with him. Simon called on Jesus as Savior and claimed his promise of eternal life. He jumped up, shouting for joy, and ran back to the camp to tell everyone he met of the goodness of God and his power to save. Simon couldn't keep the good news a secret.

Simon already avoided many frontier vices. He did not drink, swear, gamble, or chase women. Yet becoming a believer did change his life. From that day forward Simon set aside the rifle he had carried at all times, the rifle which had sent many an Indian to his grave. Now he hiked around town with a hickory staff, his dog at his heels.

Will you be able to stand before God on Judgment Day?

19
War Declared

1811-1813

In late fall of 1811, Tecumseh traveled south from Prophetstown to convince more tribes to join his alliance. As before, he gave each allied tribe a carved post with pictograms telling what the tribes should do when his great sign, the shaking of the earth, would come. He also gave them a bundle of sticks, one for each month until the sign came. The bundles of sticks, representing months until the sign, were very small. The bundle for the Seminole tribe had just three sticks.

Before he rode away from Prophetstown, Tecumseh warned his brother he must keep the peace at all costs. The union of tribes was still too weak to defeat the enemy, even with 2,000 warriors already amassed. They must wait until the great sign came to pass.

The Prophet gave permission for some young warriors to steal a few horses, though he knew Tecumseh would not be pleased. The thieves stole five horses, and then stole the fifteen horses of the settlers who came to confront them about the theft. This gave General William Henry Harrison a good enough reason to march his army toward Prophetstown.

The Prophet requested a peace parley with Harrison for the following

General William Henry Harrison

day. Before dawn, Harrison's army heard Indian war whoops and musket fire. The nine hundred men grabbed their firearms and took cover from the surprise attack.

The Indians encircled Harrison's camp and fought valiantly. They might have triumphed if they had fought their usual way. The Prophet foretold that the bullets would not hurt them and declared that half of the whites were dead and the others were crazy. When dawn came and the Indians spied their dead comrades, they scattered. Harrison ordered Prophetstown and its food supplies burned. [17]

Simon Kenton Unlikely Hero

This defeat weakened Tecumseh's Indian confederation. His dream of winning back Indian lands, his work of the last decade, was nearly destroyed. The Prophet became an outcast. Yet Tecumseh still hoped to regain Indian territories by joining forces with the British. When the great sign came, the Indians must bring their weapons and gather at Fort Malden, on Lake Erie.

Tecumseh's great sign did come. In December of 1811 a powerful earthquake[18] shook the ground from Mexico to Canada. Indians headed to Fort Malden from all around the country.

Two more quakes, nearly as strong, followed in the next two months. The course of the Mississippi River changed and a new lake formed. Most of Simon's Missouri land was now underwater.

The year 1812 brought ominous signs of war. On the frontier, Indian attacks increased. That spring in Ohio, Indians killed fifteen settlers. On the sea, Britain used her superior navy to blockade the nation's major harbors. Again Simon and the young nation prepared for battle against a much mightier adversary.

In June of 1812, the United States declared war on Great Britain. Simon, now fifty-seven years of age, had fought in many battles. He did not want to be left behind in this clash, but his family declared he was too old. He stayed home and followed the news of the battles with interest.

Simon's hometown of Urbana was the assembly and departure point for General Hull's army to march north to invade Canada. One day a crowd of soldiers pounded on Simon's door. One man snarled that Simon harbored the enemy. The soldiers meant the two Shawnee, Chiuxca and Coonahaw, who lived on Simon's land and were his good friends. The dozen or so men planned to shoot the two Indians, the sooner the better.

Simon held up his hand, as if to say, "wait here", and went into his cabin to get the rifle he had not carried in years. He returned and walked a few steps from the house, spun around, and pointed the gun at the group. "Mebbe you'll massacre them Injens, but not whilst I'm alive." The soldiers realized that even if they did kill this brave man, some of them would die in the process. So they retreated, shaking their heads in amazement that a white man would put his life on the line for Indians.

A steady stream of Kentucky soldiers marched through Urbana, often camping for the night. These included many of Simon's old comrades in arms, so he invited them to stay at his house. The crowded conditions in the small cabin didn't bother Simon. One of his granddaughters recorded that Simon also cared for the sick and suffering among the soldiers. "He visited the camps, and if any needed assistance he gave it without wishing any recompense."

One stormy evening, Kenton tramped to town through a deep snow to see if any troops needed help. He found a company of packhorse men who had no shelter for the night. He invited them all to his home and had his womenfolk take care of the one who was sick. His generosity was hindered by the fact that he had just the basics to offer—warmth, shelter, and hominy.

Simon finally got a chance to fight in 1813 when an urgent call came for volunteers. A large force of British soldiers bombarded Fort Meigs, a key supply storehouse. If the British cannons could batter down the walls, Tecumseh and his Indians would swarm out of the woods to attack the defenders. Unless help came soon the besieged fort would fall.

Inside the fort, General William Henry Harrison had a trick up his sleeve. He ordered his men to dig a traverse, a bank of earth right behind the fort's wall to absorb the cannon fire. Simon and the volunteer rescuers came, but the enemy continued the shelling. For eight days the fort held out. Finally General Proctor and the Indians gave up.

Simon was back home in Urbana when his old friend General Shelby marched his Kentucky militia into town. Many of the men knew Simon from years gone by, so they sat around reminiscing about old times. Simon longed to join them in their march to join General Harrison's army. The men urged Simon to "come along for the fun." General Shelby encouraged him to come along as counselor and adviser.

Betsy strongly opposed the idea. She said Simon had been on enough wild adventures, he had a bad leg, and he was too old to stand the harsh conditions. But Simon's soldier son had been captured, and this might be the best chance to find out what had happened to him.[19] Besides, Simon felt as tough as ever. Would he leave with the army or listen to his wife's objections?

The Kenton clan heaved a sigh of relief when the militia marched north without Simon. The day after they left, Simon loaded a sack of corn on his horse, as if to take it to the mill. But he also collected a blanket, his rifle, powder and bullets, and stuffed some supplies inside his hunting shirt. As he headed out of town he sent word back with a neighbor to let his family know he had gone to fight against "Beast Proctor." (The British general got this nickname because he allowed his Indian allies to murder injured prisoners after battles.)

Simon easily caught up with General Shelby's troops. He recognized the route to Sandusky from his long-ago trip to Detroit with Pierre Drouillard. Simon and the other militiamen would normally march by land to Fort Malden in Canada, where Proctor and Tecumseh waited. But Commodore Oliver Hazard Perry had just won a big victory in the Battle of Lake Erie. The American troops crossed the lake by ship.

Simon enjoyed his first journey by ship. He smiled to himself as he noted details to tell Betsy and the children.

British General Proctor had prepared to meet a land assault on his position at Fort Malden. Tecumseh's 1,200 Indians stood ready to fight alongside him. When Proctor spotted the ships headed in his direction, he ordered a retreat. Tecumseh scorned this general's cowardice; twice before he had seen General Proctor retreat from battles. Tecumseh pressured him to stand and fight. But Proctor ordered the fort burned to the ground and marched his 800 mounted Redcoats north along the Thames River. Tecumseh's forces reluctantly joined the retreat.

The cause of winning back Indian lands was doomed and Tecumseh knew it. He spoke bitterly of the maltreatment of the Indians by their British allies. He advised his followers, "It is better that we should return to our own country and let the Americans come on and fight the British." Two tribes, the Chippewa and the Sioux, reminded Tecumseh that he had persuaded them to join the British and he should not leave them now. Tecumseh agreed. As long as any Indians stayed to fight, he would lead them. But by morning, more than half the Indians had taken his advice to return to their homes.

General William Henry Harrison led an army of 3,500 including General Shelby's force of Kentuckians. They pursued General Proctor and Tecumseh. Each time the British general seemed like he had chosen a spot to stop and fight, he changed his mind and kept retreating. Tecumseh threatened to abandon him unless he showed some backbone. Finally Proctor's army and Tecumseh's followers prepared for the battle beside the Thames River, with marshy ground on one **flank** and the river protecting the other flank.

The night before the battle, Tecumseh again strongly urged his fellow warriors to return home. He described the defeat awaiting them. To their great sorrow, he also foretold his own death. He told them to retreat as soon as he died, for the battle would be lost.

Now he removed all signs of rank—his medals, bracelets, and headband—and wore just a deerskin shirt and leggins. He gave away his weapons, keeping only his war club.

The Battle of the Thames, October 5, 1813, was brief, as battles go. General Harrison sent his first battalion against the Redcoats. The British lines crumbled; surrender followed.

The second battalion had a harder task, attacking the Indians in their hidden positions. Twenty brave men formed a front line of attackers and faced fire from Shawnee guns. Both sides battled fiercely for an hour, with many falling. During the battle, Tecumseh shouted to his warriors, "Be strong! Be brave!" Tecumseh charged forward, leading his men, but fell dead from a bullet in his chest. When the rest of the warriors saw their leader fall, they vanished into the woods. The soldiers searched for Indians to fight, but the battle was over.

General Harrison questioned his men whether Tecumseh had been killed in battle. The Kentuckians sent for Simon Kenton, knowing he could identify the great chief. A parade of souvenir seekers followed Simon as he walked among the three hundred fallen Indians. He recognized a buckskin-clad Shawnee as Tecumseh, but he held his tongue.

Instead he pointed to another fallen Indian, a chief with many ornaments. In a few minutes that warrior was stripped.

In the middle of the night, Shawnee warriors returned to the battleground to gather their fallen chief. They carried him to a secret place for burial. The woods around them reverberated with their doleful death chant. Shawnee still visit this secret spot in Canada to honor their great chief, considered by many to be the greatest Native American military leader.

The war lasted two more years, but neither side gained new territory. The Indians, however, lost territory. In 1817 they signed a treaty giving up most of their lands in northeast Ohio. They received annuities and ten tribal reserves for homelands.

Simon forgave his former enemies and some even became his friends. Do you think you could forgive someone who had been your enemy?

20
The Fifty-Year Reunion

1832

*S*imon Kenton had served his country well. The years after the War of 1812 brought an end to many eras of his life. Would he retire?

His friend George Rogers Clark was drinking himself to death. Simon went for one last visit to reminisce. Both recalled the times when Simon had been at Clark's side—for the daring capture of Kaskaskia, and as a scout for militia campaigns against the Shawnees.

After Clark's death in 1818 Simon determined that his friend's heroic deeds for his country would not be forgotten. Simon valued George Rogers Clark as one of the great men of his time, one who had not received the honor he deserved. In his opinion, Clark "had done more to save Kentucky from the Indians than any other man." Simon began dictating memories of his friend to his wife Betsy.

In 1819, Simon again spent time in jail for debts, this time in Kentucky. Kenton, who at one time owned nearly 400,000 acres, became poorer as his land holdings dwindled. Whenever he needed money, he traveled back to Kentucky to sell land he still owned there. During one visit to Kentucky he was arrested and jailed for non-payment of back taxes on land he had *given away*. This so angered him that he refused to pay, though he could afford it. He wouldn't let his friends pay, either. Some would call him a stubborn old man. Others would say he stood up for his principles. The jail in Washington treated their famous prisoner kindly. Simon still had the freedom to hike around the town. He visited relatives and friends, took supper at one house, and traded yarns at another.

Simon Kenton Unlikely Hero

Should this land of liberty duplicate English law and lock up a man who could not pay his debts? Using Kenton's unfair case as an example, one of Simon's friends in the state legislature campaigned for repeal of the debtor's law. Later, the Marquis de Lafayette, the famous Frenchman who fought beside George Washington in the Revolutionary War, visited the United States. When he inquired about Kenton, he was shocked to hear his Revolutionary comrade was in debtor's prison. This at last prompted the Kentucky legislature to repeal the law. In 1821, after nearly two years, Simon was again a free man.

Simon moved his wife and four children to an eighteen-foot square cabin in Zanesfield, Ohio. Nearby, abundant sugar maple trees provided sap for boiling into syrup each spring. An orchard of apple trees grew from seeds planted by Indians. A stone's throw away the Indian village of Wapatomica sparked memories of Simon's captivity. There his friend Simon Girty had rescued him from a fiery death.

Simon spent his time visiting with his friends and many relatives around Zanesfield. He told stories of his adventures as he enjoyed a bowl of hominy. Children sat on his lap so they could feel the dent in his head from the Shawnee tomahawk. After poking the fire with his walking stick, Simon often closed his eyes for a nap, undisturbed by the work of the household going on around him.

Simon and Betsy attended the Mount Tabor church not far from their home. Betsy walked two paces behind Simon, as was the custom for a wife showing respect to her husband. In pleasant weather, the meetings were held under the shade trees, with Indians and settlers worshiping together. The Indians arrived on their horses and brought along their dogs. An interpreter translated the sermons of both Indian and white preachers.

Simon had a marvelous memory for details of the major events of his lifetime. The historian Lyman Draper collected Simon's memories of battles and the famous people who were his friends or enemies. Draper's Kenton-related manuscripts fill thirteen volumes. Many other men came to visit Simon in his later years to collect information for histories of the frontier or a Kenton biography.[20]

In 1832, Simon looked forward to the fifty-year reunion of the men still alive from George Rogers Clark's Indian campaign of 1782. Clark and most of the army were gone. Fewer than fifty men were left, and only fifteen of them could come. Simon widened the celebration to include "the Citizens of the Western Country", those pioneers who had helped in the conquest. They were invited to meet on November 4 at old Fort Washington, near Cincinnati. They would "attend divine service" and "meet . . . friends . . . and then take a final adieu, to meet no more, until we shall all meet in a world of spirits."

Simon and Betsy set out on a trip to Kentucky before the reunion. Simon's witness was necessary in a legal battle over a land boundary, so they traveled in style. He had travel allowance of "fifty dollars and expenses both ways." They traveled to Dayton by carriage, Simon in his greatcoat and Betsy in her best "brown cassamere with green spots and a green silk . . . bonnet." From Dayton, they traveled by stage to Cincinnati, and then by steamboat to old Limestone and Washington. The one hundred forty miles made a long, tiring journey for Simon, then 77 years of age, and Betsy, 54. Yet the time was well spent. Betsy wrote down the memories of George Rogers Clark which filled Simon's heart as the reunion neared.

Simon, as part of his court testimony, hiked to the land in dispute. Crowds of citizens came along just to see the famous General Kenton. He pointed to a tree that marked the corner of the disputed property. Long ago they had used it for target practice, shooting at a mark. The crowd tramped over to the tree, cut and scraped the bark, and found Simon's lead bullet still resting there. The case was now settled, thanks to the old general's remarkable memory.

Simon and Betsy headed next to Cincinnati for the fifty-year reunion. Though few of the original men were left, many others sent word they planned to come. But an unexpected enemy spoiled the plans. **Cholera** swept through the country. Fear of the disease caused all plans for the celebration to be cancelled overnight. As you might expect, Simon took this disappointment in stride.

Simon Kenton Unlikely Hero

On the way home, Simon and Betsy took a side trip to Chillicothe Old Town. Friends and family honored the old general at a reception there. Crowds retraced with him that first grueling gauntlet run.

For the last leg of their journey home the Kentons traveled by a "two-horse **hack**." The young man who rode with them later penned his impressions of his travel-mates.

"I found . . . a very elderly and dignified gentleman, who at the first glance commanded my respect. We chatted . . . he pointed out the path along which the Indians had once escorted him, a prisoner . . . to make him run the gauntlet. [He told me of] his early hardships in the backwoods and adventures with the Indians. At the time I didn't take any hint as to who he was . . . [but when we arrived at Urbana] the people collected . . . around the hack, all anxious to see and speak to . . . a man of eminent distinction . . . I soon learned I had been traveling with [one] who I had till then known only in history—the celebrated pioneer, Simon Kenton, and his excellent lady."

By the Providence of God Simon Kenton escaped death from bullets, tomahawks, fire, and disease. He used his woodsman's skills to help others survive on the dangerous Kentucky frontier. As his health declined, Simon reminisced more often about those early years. At eighty-one years of age, Simon had outlived his closest friends—Simon Girty, Daniel Boone, and George Rogers Clark. In 1836, with his wife Betsy at his side, Simon drew the final breath of his eventful life.

After his death, two states vied for the honor of placing a monument over his remains. (Ohio won and their monument stands in Urbana.) Kenton's name lives on in many place names in Kentucky and Ohio. The beautiful new Simon Kenton Bridge arches over the river between Ohio and Kentucky. Many organizations name their chapter after this fearless frontiersman. Simon's many descendants and kinsmen gather in Washington and Maysville (formerly Limestone), Kentucky for the annual Simon Kenton Festival. They keep alive the memory of the reckless young man who turned out to be a remarkable pathfinder, guide, protector, role model, and friend.

Do you think you would make a good pioneer, able to endure all the hardships?

Glossary of Unfamiliar Terms

blockhouse. Fortified log structure two stories high with portholes for guns.

camp meeting. Outdoor religious gathering lasting for many days.

cede. To surrender ownership.

cholera. Intestinal disease caused by contaminated water or food, which may cause death.

commonwealth. An independent territory governed for the common good of the residents.

Conestoga wagon. A heavy wagon with a canvas top and large wheels, pulled by oxen or horses.

corncrib. Building for storing corn.

cut-ta-ho-tha. Shawnee word for one condemned to death, especially by burning at the stake.

flank. One side of a military formation.

frigate. Large fighting ship.

gauntlet. Double line of Indians wielding weapons, through which their prisoners must run.

hack. An enclosed carriage for hire, pulled by two or four horses.

heifer. Young female cow.

hominy. Corn softened by soaking in ash-water, used for making corn-based foods.

intelligence. Information of military importance.

irons in the fire. Iron rods in the blacksmith's fire, heated before making a finished product. Too many irons in the fire mean some are ready but cannot be worked before they cool or melt.

leggins. Leather leg coverings, often of deer hide, to protect the legs from brush, briars, and snakes. They are also called Indian stockings.

locator. Surveyor who finds, measures, and marks property.

long hunt. Extended trip in the wilderness during which hunters travel long distances and harvest furs to sell back in civilizaton.

long knives. Nickname for American soldiers because they carried swords.

man-of-war. Large fighting ship.

Middle Ground. One of many names for the state we now call Kentucky. Other names were Can-tuc-kee, Canelands, and Cain-tuck.

militia. Civilians who are called up to fight as soldiers when needed, usually less dependable than a regular army.

palisade. Wall of pointed logs around the perimeter of a fort.

parole. Release of a prisoner on his sworn promise not to fight again.

plat. To mark out a property, often into lots for a town.

Providence of God. The belief that all events are divinely planned for God's purposes.

renegade. One who turns from his original loyalty, a traitor.

six-pounder. Cannon that fires cannon balls measuring three and a half inches across, weighing six pounds.

speculator. One who hopes to get rich by buying something cheaply and selling it for much more.

station. Fortified settlement on the frontier, usually civilian rather than military.

swamp fever. Malaria, transmitted by mosquitoes, characterized by recurring chills and fevers.

tenant farm. Rented farm with landlord taking part of the yearly crop.

trace. Path marked on trees and chopped through the wilderness, often following paths made by animals such as buffalo.

vermilion. Bright red paint used by Indians.

wampum belt. Woven band of beads, about four inches wide by thirty-six inches long, with figures and colors representing important points to be remembered in a speech or treaty.

warrant. Document issued by the government as a reward for military service, allowing the holder to claim or buy land.

wegiwa. Shawnee pole and bark house.

Time Line

April 3, 1755—Simon Kenton, seventh child of Mary and Mark Kenton, is born in Fauquier County, Virginia.

April 10, 1771—Simon Kenton fights William Leachman, flees to escape justice.

November 2, 1771—Simon Kenton, George Strader, and John Yeager set out by canoe down the Ohio on a long hunt. First time in Kentucky.

March 19, 1773—Simon Kenton and George Strader escape from Indian attack on their camp, near present-day Charleston, WV.

October, 1774—Simon Kenton scouts for the militia in Dunmore's War against the Shawnee.

October 10, 1774—Battle of Point Pleasant; Kentucky militia under Colonel Lewis defeat the Indians under Chief Cornstalk.

March, 1775—Simon Kenton and Thomas Williams finally locate the cane lands and settle near Washington, Kentucky.

April 19, 1775—British Redcoats march against colonial minutemen in Lexington, Massachusetts.

June 6, 1776—Two Kentucky men chosen to beg powder and lead from the Virginia Assembly for defense against Indian attacks.

April 24, 1777—First of three sieges of Boonesborough. Simon saves Daniel Boone from death.

July 4, 1778—Kenton scouts for Colonel George Rogers Clark when he captures the British post of Kaskaskia.

September 1778—Simon Kenton is captured by Shawnees and condemned to die.

Simon Kenton Unlikely Hero

June 1779—Simon Kenton escapes captivity in Detroit.

June 1780—Captain Bird and his army of British Rangers and Indians, about 700 total, attack Ruddell's and Martin's Stations. Both stations surrender in the face of the two cannons. The 450 prisoners spend three years as British or Indian captives.

August 1780—George Rogers Clark leads campaign against Shawnee towns of Chillicothe and Pickaway Town.

October 19, 1781—British General Cornwallis surrenders to General George Washington, effectively ending the Revolutionary War.

March 8, 1782—Pennsylvania militia massacre of 96 Christian Delaware Indians at Gnadenhutten, Ohio Territory.

August 19, 1782—British and Indian forces defeat Kentucky militia at Blue Licks, Kentucky Territory.

November 1782—George Rogers Clark again leads the Kentucky militia against Shawnee towns.

Spring of 1783—Simon returns to Virginia to bring his relatives to Kentucky.

1784—Kenton's Station blockhouse constructed.

February 1787—Simon marries Martha "Patsey" Dowden.

Children born: Martha, November 1787; John, 1790; Simon, Junior 1793; Sarah, 1795.

1794—Battle of Fallen Timbers, General Anthony Wayne defeats Indian confederation.

1795—Greenville Treaty signed, ending the Indian wars on the frontier.

1796—Martha, Simon's wife, dies in a fire.

1798—Simon marries Elizabeth "Betsy" Jarboe

Children born: Matilda 1799; Elizabeth, 1803; William, 1807; Elizabeth 1811; Ruth Jane, 1816

April, 1799—The Kenton family moves to Springfield, in Ohio territory.

1805—Thomas Jefferson doubles the size of the nation with the Louisiana Purchase from France.

1805—Simon promoted to Brigadier General of militia.

1805—Kenton spends a year in jail in Urbana, Ohio.

1806—Tecumseh gathers followers from many tribes at Greenville, Ohio.

1810—Kentons move to Urbana, Ohio.

November 1811—Battle of Tippecanoe, Indians defeated by General William Henry Harrison.

December, 1811—New Madrid earthquake, Tecumseh's great sign.

June, 1812—America declares war on Great Britain.

October 5, 1813, Battle of the Thames—American armies defeat British and Indians; Tecumseh is killed in battle.

1819-1821—Simon in debtor's prison in Kentucky.

1821—Kenton family moves to Zanesfield.

1832—Fifty-year reunion scheduled for George Rogers Clark's 1782 army.

1836—Simon Kenton dies with Betsy at his side.

Bibliography for Simon Kenton, Unlikely Hero

Callaway, Rex. *Tomahawks and Treaties, Micajah Callaway and the Struggle for the Ohio River Valley.* Franklin, TN: American History Press, 2010.

Clark, Thomas D. *Simon Kenton, Kentucky Scout.* New York: Reprint of 1943 Farrar and Rinehart edition, Jesse Stuart Foundation: Ashland, KY, 1993.

Clark, Thomas D., editor. *The Voice of the Frontier, John Bradford's Notes on Kentucky.* Lexington: University of Kentucky, 1993.

Crain, Ray. *Simon Kenton, "The Great Frontiersman".* Urbana, OH: Main Graphics, 1992.

Crain, Ray. *The Land Beyond the Mountains.* Urbana, OH: Main Graphics, 1994.

De Haas, Wills. *History of the Early Settlement and Indian Wars of Western Virginia.* Wheeling, WV: H. Hoblitzell, 1851.

Eckert, Allan W. *A Sorrow in our Heart.* New York, NY: Smithmark Publishers, Inc., 1992.

Eckert, Allan W. *The Frontiersmen, a Narrative.* Boston, MA: Little, Brown, and Company, 1967.

Giles, Janice Holt. *The Kentuckians.* Reprint of 1953 Houghton Mifflin Company edition, University Press of Kentucky, Lexington, KY: 1987.

Heath, William. *William Wells and the Struggle for the Old Northwest.* Norman, OK: University of Oklahoma Press, 2015.

Hildreth, S.P. *Pioneer History: Being and Account of the First Examinations of the Ohio Valley, and the Early Settlement of the Northwest Territory.* Cincinnati, OH: H.W. Derby & Co. Publishers, 1848.

Hintzen, William. *A Sketchbook of The Border Wars of the Upper Ohio Valley: (1769-1794) Conflicts and Resolutions.* Manchester, CT: Precision Shooting, Inc., 1999.

Jahns, Patricia. *The Violent Years: Simon Kenton and the Ohio-Kentucky Frontier.* New York: Hastings House, 1962.

Kenton, Edna. *Simon Kenton, His Life and Period, 1755-1836.* Garden City, NJ: The Country Life Press, 1930.

McDonald, John. *Biographical Sketches of General Nathaniel Massie, General Duncan McArthur, Captain William Wells, and General Simon Kenton: Who Were Early Settlers in the Western Country.* Cincinnati, OH: E. Morgan and Son, 1838.

Schmidt, Ethan A. *Native Americans in the American Revolution, How the War Divided, Devastated, and Transformed the Early American Indian World.* Santa Barbara, CA: Praeger an imprint of ABC-CLIO, LLC, 2014.

Stockwell, Mary. *The Other Trail of Tears, The Removal of the Ohio Indians.* Yardley, PA: Westholme Publishing, LLC, 2014.

Thom, James Alexander. *Long Knife, A Novel Based on the Life of George Rogers Clark.* New York: Ballantine Books, 1979.

WEBSITES
frontierfolk.org/kenton
More information on Simon Kenton and the frontier life researched by a Kenton descendant
TheKentonKin.wordpress.com
In honor and memory of our Kenton ancestors and their friends.

Endnotes

1. How did Kentucky get its name? The name has Native American origin, with several tribes having words sounding like Kentucky. In the eighteenth century, people spelled a word by sounding it out. Kentucky's name has been variously spelled Cane-tuck-ee, Can-tucky, Kain-tuck-ee and Kentuckee. The current boundaries are nearly the same as the original region.
2. All three later spent time in prison for these and other treasonous activities.
3. People tried to take everything they would need in the wilderness because so few items were available, and those were very expensive.
4. One old friend even came to stay—Simon's rescuer of long ago, Peter Drouillard.
5. Martha "Patsey" bore five children to Simon

    1787—Nancy

    1790—John

    1793—Simon, Junior

    1795—Sarah

    1796—unnamed
6. Simon Girty became a renegade in 1778.
7. One historian states that not even Custer's Last Stand could come close to equaling it.
8. Judging by the symptoms, this was probably malaria.
9. Tribes included Wyandot, Shawnee, Ojibwe, Potowatomie, Miami, Kickapoo, Kaskaskia, Wabash confederacy, Cherokee, and Delaware.

10. A peace wampum belt was usually five inches wide and three to six feet long.

11. General Wayne clearly explained the boundary line between Indian and lands of the United States. The Indians ceded 25,000 square miles of territory to the government, as well as sixteen six-mile-square regions inside the Indian territory. Each of the twelve tribes would receive goods worth $1,666.00, and annual payments of $825.00. The tribes would still have hunting and fishing privileges throughout the Ohio country.

12. Spain ruled this new frontier at that time.

13. Elizabeth (Betsy) bore five children to Simon;

    1799—Matilda

    1803—Elizabeth

    1807—William

    1811—Elizabeth

    1816—Ruth Jane

14. One quotation from Tecumseh: "These lands are ours . . . no one has the right to remove us because we were the first owners; the Great Spirit above has appointed this place for us on which to light our fires, and here we will remain."

15. Daniel Boone's famous trace marked the trail from Virginia through the Cumberland Gap to Kentucky.

16. Kenton spent much of this money to buy a tract of land on the Mississippi near New Madrid, Missouri, a beautiful spot he and Betsy could retire to. But Tecumseh's sign, the 1811 earthquake estimated at 7.5 magnitude, was centered in New Madrid. It shook five states, formed a huge lake, and made tens of thousands of acres disappear, including nearly all of Simon's land.

17. Tippecanoe, the site of the battle, became Harrison's nickname and part of his slogan for his campaign for president in 1840.

18. On December 16, 1811, the first of three earthquakes occurred, named the New Madrid earthquakes for New Madrid, Missouri. The U.S. Geological Survey said this earthquake was close to 10 times stronger than the one that destroyed San Francisco in the late 1800s. The massive quake caused such a major shift of seismic plates that it was said church bells rang out in Boston, sidewalks cracked in Washington, D.C., forests disappeared, lakes were created, villages were swallowed, and for a few hours the Mississippi River ran backwards.

19. Kenton still had no word of his son's fate after the Battle of the Thames. The following year, Simon and Betsy received word of his death as he fought alongside Mexicans against Spain.

20. Only one man, John McClung, completed a book. He included a brief life of Simon Kenton among others in his book *Sketches of Western Adventure*. Later, Judge John James captured Simon's own eccentric manner of speaking as he took notes on Simon's stories. His notes survive, but he did not publish a book.

Image Credits

1. **Simon Kenton Portrait:** Simon Kenton Chapter of the Sons of the American Revolution, www.sksar.org Public domain.
2. **Fort Pitt at Junction of Monongahela and Allegheny Rivers:** Pennsylvania State Archives Public domain. commons.wikimedia.org/wiki/File:Fort_Pitt_in_1776.jpg
3. **Battle of Point Pleasant:** Project Gutenberg. Public domain. commons.wikimedia.org/wiki/File:Battle_of_point_pleasant.jpg
4. **Daniel Boone Led Settlers Overland to Kentucky:** Gift of Nathaniel Phillips, 1890. Public domain. commons.wikimedia.org/wiki/File:George_Caleb_Bingham_-_Daniel_Boone_escorting_settlers_through_the_Cumberland_Gap.jpg
5. **Fort Boonesborough:** Clark County Public Library; G.W. Ranck's Boonesborough published in 1901; Image, The Filson Historical Society, Kentucky. Public domain.
6. **Simon Kenton Saving Daniel Boone's Life:** Courtesy Mingusboodle. Public domain. commons.wikimedia.org/wiki/File%3ASimon_Kenton_rescuing_Daniel_Boone.jpg
7. **Fur Trade with the Indians:** Library and Archives Canada—originally from: Cartouche from William Faden, "A map of the Inhabited Part of Canada from the French Surveys; with the Frontiers of New York and New England", 1777. Public domain. commons.wikimedia.org/wiki/File:Fur_traders_in_canada_1777.jpg
8. **Clark Leads a Surprise Winter Attack on Vincennes:** *The Hero of Vincennes: The Story of George Rogers Clark,* by Lowell Thomas. Public domain. commons.wikimedia.org/wiki/File:March_to_Vincennes.jpg
9. **Shawnee Warriors:** Courtesy Photojunkie. Public domain. commons.wikimedia.org/wiki/File:Indian_Warriors,_Fort_Pitt_Museum_Display.jpg
10. **Flatboat on the Ohio:** Engraving by Alfred Waud from The Historic New Orleans Collection. Public domain. commons.wikimedia.org/wiki/File:Traveling-by-flatboat-engraving-by-Alfred-R-Waud.png
11. **Conestoga Wagon:** Courtesy Pearson Scott Foresman. Public domain. commons.wikimedia.org/wiki/File:Prairie_schooner_(PSF).png
12. **General "Mad Anthony" Wayne:** Library of Congress. Public domain. wikimedia.org/wiki/File:Anthony_Wayne.jpg
13. **Wampum Belt:** © Tidridge, under license CC4.0. commons.wikimedia.org/wiki/File:Covenant_Chain_Wampum.jpg
14. **Louisiana Purchase Showing Current State Boundaries:** © William Morris, under license CC4.0. commons.wikimedia.org/wiki/File:Louisiana_Purchase.png
15. **Camp Meeting:** Association of Religion Data Archives, Barton Stone preaching at Cane Ridge Camp Meeting by Robert Stuart Sanders. Public domain. thearda.com/timeline/events/event_239.asp
16. **General William Henry Harrison:** National Portrait Gallery, Smithsonian Institution. Public domain. commons.wikimedia.org/wiki/William_Henry_Harrison#/media/File:William_H._Harrison.jpg
17. **George Rogers Clark, Kentucky Militia Leader:** Indiana State Museum and Historic Sites
18. **Blockhouse:** by Aaron Crute
19. **Longrifle:** Photo by Bob Meyer
20. **Tomahawk; Long Knife; Chief Logan; Six-pounder Cannon; Indian Pictograms and Their Meanings; Kentucky Circa 1800; Clark's Expedition to British-held Kaskaskia; Early Settlements and Indian Villages; Settlements Along the Ohio River; Clark's Campaign Against the Shawnee; Northwest Territory, Showing Current State Boundaries; Prophetstown, Fort Malden, and the Battle of the Thames:** by Karen Meyer
21. **Chief Tecumseh:** © ivan-96 | iStock
22. **Indian Buffalo Hunt:** © bauhaus1000 | iStock
23. **Millstone:** © cheri131 | iStock
24. **Pioneer Cabin:** © duncan1890 | iStock

What others are saying about Kenton's biography

Boone Morrison, 4x great grandson of Daniel Boone

Karen Meyer has done it again with this new title on the life of one of the major figures in the settlement of the Colonial frontier. Thrown into an adventurous life at an early age, Simon Kenton gained a place in history as the frontier developed.

Karen has caught the flavor of the tumultuous times and events and the personalities who were close to Kenton in this book aimed at the Middle School reader. Middle School literature teachers speak of how difficult it is to find books for this age level that appeal to young boys and the author has perfectly hit that spot.

Highly recommended to any young reader, or their teachers.

Marc Faulkner, Assistant Editor The Kenton Kin Association www.thekentonkin.wordpress.com

I personally have to say that I love, love, love what you are doing with this project!!! I have read three Simon Kenton books (Eckert, Kenton and Clark-along with hours upon hours of internet research while putting together the Kenton Kin's new website) in the last year, so I have a fair point of reference. It is easy to see that you have researched your subject well and I appreciate that you are making every effort to keep things historically accurate.

I know I speak for all of the Kenton Kin Association, when I say we take our family history seriously. As a group "the primary objective of our organization shall be to promote the life and deeds of General Simon Kenton, frontiersman, scout and protector of early Kentucky. To promote Kenton genealogy. Encourage family unity and fellowship. Preserve Kenton artifacts and historical accuracy.» In this regard, you have hit a home run and I am behind your project 100% - I support what you are doing all the way!

Sawyer Gorney, 4th Grade Student, Colorado

* * * * * I rate this book five stars. Never a dull moment, and I couldn't put it down. It is a detailed story of a little-known American hero.

*The author wishes to thank Jon Hagee
(6x great-nephew of Simon Kenton) for his many
detailed suggestions on the manuscript.
To the many others who read and gave feedback—Janet Shay, Julie Geist, Sawyer Gorney,
Nicole Smith, Robert Meyer—thank you!*

CPSIA information can be obtained
at www.ICGtesting.com
Printed in the USA
BVHW012052230622
640494BV00003B/141